5 10770

SEEING *Red,*
FEELING *Blue,*
OR IN THE *Pink*

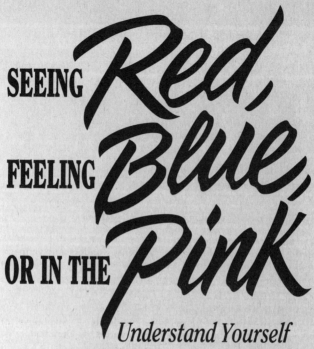

*Understand Yourself
Better Through a Colorful
Analysis of Your Emotions*

Tonya & Mark Pantle

ZondervanPublishingHouse
Grand Rapids, Michigan

A Division of HarperCollinsPublishers

P9-DTM-184

Seeing Red, Feeling Blue, or in the Pink
Copyright © 1993 by Tonya and Mark Pantle
All rights reserved

Requests for information should be directed to:
Zondervan Publishing House
Grand Rapids, Michigan 49530

Library of Congress Cataloging-in-Publication Data

Pantle, Tonya T.
    Seeing red, feeling blue, or in the pink : understand yourself better
through a colorful analysis of your emotions / Tonya T. and Mark L.
Pantle.
        p. cm.
    Includes bibliographical references.
    ISBN 0-310-48251-8 (pbk.)
    1. Emotions—Religious aspects—Christianity. 2. Symbolism of
colors—Miscellanea. 3. Self-report inventories. 4. Christian
life—1960– I. Pantle, Mark L. II. Title.
BV4597.3.P36   1993
248.4—dc20   93-22760
                                                                 CIP
                                                                  AC

Edited by Bruce and Becky Durost Fish
Cover design by Dennis Hill Art Design
Photo of authors by Joelle Pantle

Printed in the United States of America

93 94 95 96 97 / DH / 5 4 3 2 1

To the other generations who share our home:
Joelle, Matthew, Barbara, Joe, and Granny

Contents

——Introduction——
Color Me Fascinated

Have you ever wondered why you feel blue when you are sad, see red when angry, or turn green with envy?

Colors have been associated with emotions since people first toiled under the yellow sun and slept beneath the dark blue sky. In fact, color analysis was around long before the "Color Me Beautiful"[1] trend had everyone rushing to have skin, hair, and eye tones evaluated. Through the ages, color has been analyzed for a variety of purposes: to try to predict the future, to describe personalities, to improve appearances, and even to attempt physical healing.

This book presents what may be the most important color analysis of all: that of our "inside colors." These are the colors that reflect our emotional (and thus our physical, mental, and spiritual) condition. Our color analysis identifies your emotional colors and then shows you how to understand and take charge of them. Just as a typical color analysis advises how to create a balanced, coordinated appearance, our emotional color analysis indicates where feelings are imbalanced and suggests ways to put you in the pink.

In the next eleven chapters we show you how to find your emotional vulnerabilities and apply practical ways to handle them. And the good news about an emotional color analysis is that you can change your colors—at their roots!

OUR COLORFUL EMOTIONS

Perhaps because both color and emotions represent energy and life, they form a natural association. Colors themselves also create emotional reactions in us: in general, warm hues bring a sense of excitement, while cool colors create a feeling of calmness. Out of the connection between color and emotions has come a variety of colorful sayings and symbols to describe our feelings. Let's look at these phrases and their connection to the next eleven chapters.

Seeing Red: Anger

When we see red, we are angry. Anger is one of the least understood emotions, possibly because many of us have been taught from childhood that anger is a sin. By itself, however, anger is never a wrong reaction, and it is indeed a correct response when we become angry for the right reasons. In this chapter we look at the two sides of anger—righteous and not-so-righteous—and at the appropriate handling of each. We examine effective and ineffective ways both to deal with anger and to communicate it.

Feeling Blue: Sadness

The colloquial meaning of blue connotes sadness. In this chapter we discuss loss and the feelings of sadness that accompany it. We show how to use sadness to bring about healing, and we speculate on the reasons that God allows suffering and sorrow.

A Purple Rage: Bitterness and Depression

Because our complexions seem to take on a violet tinge when we seethe inside, rage is associated with purple. The rage we address in this chapter on psychological depression and bitterness is an internal product of unresolved anger (red) and sadness (blue). We look at how bitterness and depression develop and what we can do to deal effectively with them.

A Streak of Yellow: Fear

Since the mid-nineteenth century, yellow has been an American colloquialism for "cowardly." Reasons for the association of yellow with cowardliness may lie in yellow's connection with sickliness and consequent lack of vigor. This chapter explores the roots of fear and gives practical strategies to overcome it.

Turning Green: Envy

Have you ever felt sick with envy? This deadly emotion has the power to tint our complexions green as it fills us with its poison. What drives us to hurt even ourselves in our envious crusade to keep another from besting us? What underlies our need to compare ourselves to others and come out on top? In this chapter we look at envy's causes and cures.

Seeing Red, Feeling Blue, or in the Pink

Driven by the Orange Flames: Urgency

Orange takes its feeling of urgency from the consuming fire. It symbolizes hurry because of its stimulative associations. In our chapter on urgency, we show that fear (yellow) and anger (red) are the basis for urgency's orange coloring. We discuss the ill effects of the hurried and harried existence and share strategies that can enable all of us to take back control of our lives.

A World Darkened by Black: Guilt

Black has been associated with evil since ancient times. It also represents the absence of light. We use black to represent guilt because of its relationship to sin and because guilt shuts out the light of God's forgiveness, bringing darkness to the life of a Christian. In this chapter we show how to know both the fact and feeling of forgiveness.

In the Pink: Good Health

In Shakespeare's time, pink personified perfection. When he wrote "the very pink of courtesy," Shakespeare was describing the utmost politeness. As a saying, "in the pink" connotes good health. In this chapter we explain our definition of good health and its twelve characteristics. We hope that as you read this book, "in the pink" will become a part of your personal color vocabulary and your Christian life.

ONE
Understanding Our Colorful Emotions

A freckled, blond boy, kneeling beside his bed, was heard to utter this prayer: "And help me be good even when I don't feel up to it."

That boy was Dennis the Menace, but you can probably identify with his concern. How often we find our emotions in conflict with the ways we want to behave and think! If we could only feel loving, how much easier it would be to love our neighbors and our spouse. If we could only feel holy, how much easier it would be to think godly thoughts.

Before we begin to study specific emotions, however, we need a foundation to understand our colorful feelings.[1] In this chapter, we cover the what, why, and how of emotions. Then chapter two shows how to identify your own emotional colors, and chapter three presents effective and ineffective ways to change your colors. Although you may be tempted to turn immediately to a chapter dealing with a specific emotion, we encourage you to read these chapters first. Then continue with the chapter order of your preference.

THE WHAT OF EMOTIONS

Emotions have three major characteristics: they are *energy*, they are *reactions*, and they indicate *investment*.

Imagine you are hiking in the hills, and ahead of you is a squinty-eyed rattlesnake. Because you know something about rattlesnakes, your brain sounds the fear alarm to your body, which responds with an increased supply of adrenalin and an elevation in blood pressure and heart rate. This is a self-protective response: it prepares you for fight or flight. (In this case, we hope you choose flight.) You have been energized for action because emotions are *energy*. Can you think of a time when you were so angry or envious that you felt as if you could burst? That is energy building up inside your body; energy that needs a healthy and productive release.

The second characteristic of our emotions is that they are *reactions*. Feelings never show up uninvited; they arrive in the company of our thinking and behavior. If the roots of a tree represent our thinking and its trunk and branches represent our behavior, then its apples are our emotions. Our feelings of love, anger, guilt, and so on are the fruit stemming from our thinking and behavior. If we try to simply pluck off an apple of envy, another will replace it. We cannot effectively change our feelings by direct attack. Instead we need to deal with the sources behind the emotional reaction. We literally need to go to the root—along with the trunk and branches—of the problem.

Emotions can also be reactions to internal, biochemical states, independent of thinking and behavior. Perhaps you have heard the term "chemical imbalance" in reference to depression. Disorders in the body's chemistry can create emotional disorders, such as depression, anxiety, or elation. Changing emotions that arise from biochemical factors requires a change in the biochemistry, which is usually accomplished by medication. Even in these situations, however, changes in thinking and behavior are part of the therapy.

Third, our emotions indicate *investment*. Emotions arise from a sense of investment, a sense that we have something at stake. For example, if you are in a room and someone begins to kick an empty chair, you might not get too emotional about it. But if you are sitting in that chair, your feelings would quickly rise to the occasion: someone is kicking *your* chair. The intensity of your emotion will increase in proportion to your sense of investment. If you are strongly attached to your choice of seating and do not want to move, you will become more upset than if you were ready to leave anyway. That is why we get angriest at our loved ones— we have invested much of ourselves in them.

People who in general have the greatest levels of investment also tend to feel the greatest intensity of emotions. Our eleven-year-old daughter puts all of herself into whatever she does. As a result, she is quickly and intensely emotional. But have you ever known someone who glides through life on an even emotional keel, seldom getting too excited about anything? Often these folks have an "easy come, easy go" philosophy, seldom investing themselves too much in any one thing, seldom getting too stirred up in their spirits.

THE WHY OF EMOTIONS

Few of us were born with silver spoons in our mouths. All of us, however, were born with paint boxes in our heads. Your paint box is found in a spot called the limbic system, which is the area of the brain God created for your colorful emotions. God made you with the capacity to feel both pleasant and unpleasant emotions. Your paint box has cups for red (anger), blue (sadness), yellow (fear), and a myriad of other colors. When your paintbrush seems to be stuck in the blue or yellow cup, you may find yourself asking, "Why did God create me with emotions, anyway?" We would like to offer four basic reasons.

1. Our emotions are based on the nature of our relationship with God.

Recall the connection between emotions and investment: our feelings arise from a sense of investment. According to Romans 14:8, God created us to belong to him. For you to truly belong to God, you must be invested in that relationship. That investment necessitates your capacity for feelings. Without feelings, there could be no investment. Without investment, you could not belong to God. Emotions come as a package deal with belonging to God. Because God created us to belong to him, he created us with the capacity to feel.

2. Our emotions are the energy to motivate us.

We discover in Romans 7:4 that one of the reasons we belong to God is so that we can serve him. Emotions are energy; if we did not feel, we would have no drive to

14

get out of bed in the morning, no impetus to serve God. When we experience emotional energy, however, we have to find channels for it. When we feel joyful, we might be motivated to praise God for what he has done in our lives. When we feel sorrowful, we might be led to pray for God's help. When we feel angry, we might want to right a wrong.

But what about the times when we feel crippled by fear or paralyzed by depression? What has happened to the emotional energy? When emotional pain continues over a long period of time, our bodies attempt to adapt. Our emotions become blunted, and we may no longer experience emotional energy.

This experience can be compared to someone who has a stone in her shoe. At first the stone hurts her foot terribly. But if it is not removed, her foot eventually adapts to the pain until the stone is no longer felt. When you are chronically depressed or anxious, your body protects you from the energy that is not being channeled. In order to deal with the fear or depression, then, you must return to the pain and energy that first accompanied your feelings. Just as that stone would be felt anew if the foot were shifted around in the shoe, you must shift into a new perspective to look at your pain. This process is usually best accomplished with the help of a skilled counselor.

3. *Our emotions are indicators of our spiritual condition.*

Remember, emotions are reactions. When we feel a certain way, we need to search out the root of that feeling: what thinking and behavior precipitated my emotion? If your paint box is overflowing with angry red pigment, it is time to pry off the lid on the paint box and see what is underneath the tin cup that holds the red paint. What does your anger indicate about your spiritual condition? What thinking and behavior need to be examined?

One of the best indicators that you need to open your paint box is when you experience an emotional response out of proportion to an event. For example, if you are typically even-tempered and suddenly find yourself out of control because of a relatively small incident, you need to find out what hurts are buried beneath the red tin cup in your paint box.

Friends of ours were over for dinner one night when the conversation turned to the different states where we each have lived. Suddenly the husband jumped up and began screaming at his wife, recounting the difficulties he had experienced because she refused to move back to New York with him. He was as bewildered at his reaction as she was. Clearly he had buried hurts that needed to be addressed.

4. Our emotions are a reflection of God's image in us.

As image-bearers of God, we share his emotional nature. Perhaps you have never thought about God in these terms before. Do you picture God as a stern father, forever frowning over the faults of his children? Instead, we find in the Bible a picture of a God who laughs, who loves, who weeps, and who grieves. Let's look at just a few of the emotions the Bible attributes to God.

Jealousy—Exodus 20:5 tells us that our heavenly Father is jealously possessive of his children and warns us against giving our first love to anyone else. Just as an ardent lover would protect his beloved, God is intolerant of rivalry or unfaithfulness.

Anger—In Exodus 32:10 we find out how God feels when his children are unfaithful. Here God asks Moses to leave him alone so that his anger "may burn." We should not be surprised at the passion behind God's anger; how do you feel when you have been betrayed? God's justice, in fact, requires anger. He would not be a just and fair God if he simply turned his head when his children disobeyed. Justice requires an expression of displeasure when disobedience occurs.

Hate—Again, we see the passion of God's emotions in Proverbs 6:16. This passage describes seven things that God hates: things we should also hate because they stem from evil.

Love—Although God experiences the feelings of love just as we do, his love goes beyond the emotion itself. 1 John 4:8 tells us that God *is* love. God demonstrated this perfect love by sending his own Son to die for us. He calls us to be rooted and established in this same love, a love so great that it surpasses knowledge (Eph. 3:17–19).

Lust—While we usually think of lust in terms of sexual desire, the word is a translation of the Greek verb *epithumeo* and has other meanings. For example, in Luke 22:15 lust refers to a strong desire for good. Here Jesus says to his disciples, "I have eagerly desired [epithumeo] to eat this Passover with you before I suffer." Again we see the intensity of emotions felt by our Lord.

Loneliness—Whenever you think you are alone in the way you feel, remember Jesus. We are told in Mark 14:34 that while waiting to be arrested in the Garden of Gethsemane, Jesus was "overwhelmed with sorrow to the point of death." Luke 22:44 adds that his sweat was like drops of blood falling to the ground because his anguish was so great. Soon he would be nailed to the cross and experience separation from his own Father while he suffered for our sin.

On that cross Jesus felt every negative emotion we have ever endured.[2] We need to remember we are never alone in our feelings because we have a Lord who feels with us. Just as Jesus experienced our feelings of fear, sadness, and sorrow on the cross, he bears them with us today.

THE HOW OF EMOTIONAL EXPRESSION

Have you ever noticed how freely most children express their feelings? As soon as our son, Matthew, could string words together, he would tell us how he felt. When he could not have a cookie, he would say, "I feel sad." Whenever we hurt his feelings, he was quick to point it out. Matthew knew his feelings were safe with his parents; we would never scold or tease him for sharing them with us. But as our eight-year-old gains more experience in the things of the world, he is likely to find others who are not so willing to accept his feelings. As he grows up, he may find that others frown on his expression of emotions.

A common response when others reject our feelings is to "stuff" them inside, where no one can pull them out and hurt us. The problem with stuffing is that it can make us sick. Remember that emotions are energy? Stuffing emotions, then, fills our bodies with energy. With no healthy outlet for expression, the energy builds up and then attacks our body, usually at its weakest points.

This short-circuiting or suppressing of our emotions can be translated into real physical illness and can be expressed in ways we least expect.[3] This is not to say, however, that all or even the majority of physical illnesses result from emotional distress. Many conditions exist and worsen without any underlying emotional conflict.

Another problem with stuffing emotions is that after burying them over a period of time, we discover we can no longer identify how we feel. Unearthing our emotions is too painful a prospect. We cannot put a handle on how we feel; instead we have a vague sense of discomfort.

While stuffing emotions is an ineffective and malignant way to deal with them, so is its opposite: dumping. The process of dumping is more complex, however, in that it involves at least two people: the "dumper" and the "dumpee." Whenever a dumper feels bad, she finds a dumpee or two and spills out all her feelings, without regard for those listening. Some dumpers are quite indiscriminate and will dump on the closest dumpee; others limit their dumping to a favorite dumpee.

The problems with dumping are twofold. First, dumpers use up their emotional energy when they dump, making themselves feel better. They never hold on to their emotional pain long enough to look at its source. Thus they can never make any lasting changes in their feelings because they never bother to probe the thoughts and behavior behind their emotions. Second, dumpers hurt their dumpees. Have you ever been flattened by a dumper? Unfortunately, most dumpees soon learn to avoid dumpers rather than confront them, enabling dumpers to leave a flattened trail behind them.

Of course, we all engage in dumping and stuffing

from time to time. Sometimes we desperately need a shoulder to cry on before we can begin to sort out our feelings. But the crying should never replace the sorting. And sometimes we need to wait to express our feelings until we gain control over them. A brisk walk or some vigorous cleaning can be a healthy response to overwhelming emotional energy. But putting off the expression of our feelings until we are in control of them is different from stuffing them inside permanently. We put them off with the understanding that we plan to deal with them shortly. The problems arise when dumping and stuffing become our primary methods of emotional expression. Neither one glorifies God nor helps us.

TWO
Discovering Our Emotional Colors

The "Emotional Color Analysis" is designed to identify emotions that you may be experiencing at this time.[1] It differentiates eight of our colorful emotions or emotion blends: anger (red), sadness (blue), depression and bitterness (purple: red plus blue), fear (yellow), envy (green), urgency (orange: red plus yellow), and guilt (black). Each feeling corresponds with a chapter in the book, easily allowing you to learn more about each one. The analysis also assesses your sense of well-being (pink).

As you analyze your emotional colors, please keep in mind that our use of color is metaphorical. If you score high on red, that means simply that you may be experiencing excessive anger. It does *not* mean you are vigorous and impulsive, which is the definition sometimes given for "reds" in color personality tests. Our color analysis uses colors simply as symbols for emotions.

Seeing Red, Feeling Blue, or in the Pink

THE EMOTIONAL COLOR ANALYSIS

For each statement, rate the degree to which it describes you. If the statement describes you extremely well, mark a 3 in the blank next to the statement. If the statement describes you moderately well, mark a 2. If the statement describes you slightly well, mark a 1. If the statement does not describe you at all, mark a 0. Answer each question as honestly as you can; the accuracy of this analysis depends upon how well you know and reveal yourself. Scoring is provided at the end of the test.

Extremely—3
Moderately—2
Slightly—1
Not at all—0

1. _____ I have a low tolerance for frustration.
2. _____ I feel a sense of emptiness and loss.
3. _____ My anger develops into hatred.
4. _____ I experience dizziness, headaches, rapid pulse, and shortness of breath.
5. _____ I resent others who are better off than I am.
6. _____ I am too busy to enjoy life right now.
7. _____ If others knew about the bad things I have done, they probably would want nothing to do with me.
8. _____ My life has purpose and meaning.
9. _____ I blame others when things go wrong.
10. _____ I have experienced a significant loss in the past year.
11. _____ I am slow to forgive others and/or myself.
12. _____ The future is scary to me.
13. _____ I dislike being around people who seem better off than I am.

14. _____ Weekends (or days off) are not a time of rest for me.
15. _____ I have a difficult time accepting forgiveness.
16. _____ I am aware of how my behavior affects others.
17. _____ Others say I have a hot temper.
18. _____ I feel a sense of grief and mourning.
19. _____ When I am wronged, I seek revenge.
20. _____ I feel that I have little control over my life.
21. _____ I wish that I were someone else.
22. _____ I don't spend enough time with God.
23. _____ My conscience bothers me.
24. _____ I have a good sense of humor.
25. _____ I firmly stand up for my rights.
26. _____ Even though I feel sad, I still have hope for the future.
27. _____ I carry grudges.
28. _____ I am an insecure person.
29. _____ I like to be the best and have the best.
30. _____ I lie awake at night thinking about all the things I have to do.
31. _____ I feel unworthy of forgiveness.
32. _____ When I give, I do not want something in return.
33. _____ I am a critical and cynical person.
34. _____ Even though I am sad about certain things, I hold no one else responsible for my problems.
35. _____ My feelings of sadness or anger can last for two weeks or more.
36. _____ I worry and fret about things.
37. _____ I compare myself to others.
38. _____ There aren't enough hours in my day.
39. _____ Thoughts of my past plague me.
40. _____ I am open, flexible, and accepting in my relationships.

SCORING

Transfer your scores below and add up the numbers in each column. Record the sums below each column. Next you will plot your scores on a graph.

A	B	C	D	E	F	G	H
1___	2___	3___	4___	5___	6___	7___	8___
9___	10___	11___	12___	13___	14___	15___	16___
17___	18___	19___	20___	21___	22___	23___	24___
25___	26___	27___	28___	29___	30___	31___	32___
33___	34___	35___	36___	37___	38___	39___	40___
Sum___	___	___	___	___	___	___	___

PLOTTING

Plot your score for each column on the graph and shade in each section. You can use colored pencils for shading to make the visual even more graphic. Our sample shows scores of 8 for Red, 3 for Blue, 10 for Purple, 8 for Yellow, 11 for Green, 6 for Orange, 4 for Black, and 7 for Pink.

A = Red (Anger)
B = Blue (Sadness)
C = Purple (Bitterness and Depression)
D = Yellow (Fear)
E = Green (Envy)
F = Orange (Urgency)
G = Black (Guilt)
H = Pink (Well-being)

Seeing Red, Feeling Blue, or in the Pink

SAMPLE COLOR ANALYSIS

A Red	B Blue	C Purple	D Yellow	E Green	F Orange	G Black	H Pink	
—	—	—	—	—	—	—	—	15
—	—	—	—	—	—	—	—	14
—	—	—	—	—	—	—	—	13
—	—	—	—	—	—	—	—	12
—	—	—	—	▓—	—	—	—	11
—	—	▓—	—	▓—	—	—	—	10
—	—	▓—	—	▓—	—	—	—	9
▓—	—	▓—	▓—	▓—	—	—	—	8
▓—	—	▓—	▓—	▓—	—	—	▓—	7
▓—	—	▓—	▓—	▓—	▓—	—	▓—	6
▓—	—	▓—	▓—	▓—	▓—	—	▓—	5
▓—	—	▓—	▓—	▓—	▓—	▓—	▓—	4
▓—	▓—	▓—	▓—	▓—	▓—	▓—	▓—	3
▓—	▓—	▓—	▓—	▓—	▓—	▓—	▓—	2
▓—	▓—	▓—	▓—	▓—	▓—	▓—	▓—	1

Discovering Our Emotional Colors

YOUR PERSONAL EMOTIONAL
COLOR ANALYSIS

A Red	B Blue	C Purple	D Yellow	E Green	F Orange	G Black	H Pink	
—	—	—	—	—	—	—	—	15
—	—	—	—	—	—	—	—	14
—	—	—	—	—	—	—	—	13
—	—	—	—	—	—	—	—	12
—	—	—	—	—	—	—	—	11
—	—	—	—	—	—	—	—	10
—	—	—	—	—	—	—	—	9
—	—	—	—	—	—	—	—	8
—	—	—	—	—	—	—	—	7
—	—	—	—	—	—	—	—	6
—	—	—	—	—	—	—	—	5
—	—	—	—	—	—	—	—	4
—	—	—	—	—	—	—	—	3
—	—	—	—	—	—	—	—	2
—	—	—	—	—	—	—	—	1

ANALYSIS

Look at your scores in relation to one another. What is your highest color? What is your lowest color? Are some grouped together? In general, your highest scores reflect those emotions you may feel most intensely at this time.

THREE

Changing Our Colors

Just as a tree is defined by its fruit (an apple tree, a cherry tree), people are often defined by their emotional nature: she's an excitable girl, he's a moody kid, she's a happy woman. Emotions, in fact, give us our very quality of life in the same way that fruit indicates the life of a tree. We are not simply robots that process information and perform on command. We have feelings about our thoughts and actions.

Sometimes, however, we prefer not to have certain feelings. Perhaps we feel bitterness instead of love toward a spouse. Or we feel depressed instead of joyful about our circumstances. Not only can our feelings cause us mental and spiritual anguish, but they can also damage our bodies. Studies have shown that every part of our body is affected by our feelings. Even our teeth are more susceptible to decay when we experience emotional tension.[1]

This chapter addresses two foundational questions: When do we need to change our feelings? And how do we go about it?

THE WHEN OF CHANGE

Happiness is a pervasive Christian theme. Songs promote it, books proclaim it, and many Christians have come to expect it. If given a choice, most of us would opt for happiness over remorse. Yet in some circumstances a happy person should be seeking emotional change while a remorseful person should not.

Many of us learned early in childhood that certain feelings are labeled good (happiness, love, joy) and that certain feelings are labeled bad (remorse, anger, guilt). But if you recall our earlier description of emotions as reactions, then it follows that feelings are neither good nor bad. Rather, what is at their root (our thinking and behavior) can be labeled good or bad.

We need to search ourselves to discover what thoughts and behavior are causing the feelings we have. If these thoughts and behavior bring us closer to God, then they could be labeled good. Change would not be indicated. But if these thoughts and behavior push us away from God, then they could be labeled bad, suggesting a need for change. We are not labeling the feelings, but the thinking and behavior behind them.

Suppose Nancy is happy because she has found the love of her life. We would be wrong to label this a good emotion—Nancy's new love is already a married man. Nancy's thinking and behavior in this matter are pushing her away from God. Conversely, if Nancy then experiences remorse over her actions, we would be wrong to label that emotion bad. In this case Nancy is remorseful over her sin, repents, and turns to God.

Basic emotions, then, are neither good nor bad. (Certain feelings, however, such as rage, envy, and bitterness, go beyond basic reactions. The Bible clearly speaks of these nurtured emotions as sinful.) A better way to label our basic emotions is as positive or negative. Positive emotions are those that are pleasant to us; negative emotions are those that are unpleasant.

Remorse, an unpleasant emotion, may stem from good thinking and behavior (sorrow over sin leading to repentance), and happiness, a pleasant emotion, may stem from bad thinking and behavior (deciding to and then engaging in an affair). An important point, then, is that experiencing basic negative emotions is *not* sinful. Rather, God can use unpleasant emotions to turn us from sin.

We cannot base our need for change upon the way we feel. Instead we must look at the effect of the thinking and behavior behind the feelings. Are we moving closer to God? Or are we pushing ourselves away from him?

THE HOW OF CHANGE

When we have determined that our emotional reactions are damaging our relationship with God (and consequently, our relationships with others), we need to begin the work of change. Changing feelings *is* work because it requires us to make fundamental changes in our thinking and behavior. It also demands that we acknowledge emotions that we may rather avoid. But if we fail to allow ourselves to experience these unpleasant emotions, then we cannot harness their energy for change.

At the end of this chapter we discuss the *foundation* for real change, and in subsequent chapters we explore the *process* of change for specific emotions. First, however, we examine two often-used strategies for dealing with emotions that seem to help. They actually *hinder* change.

Direct Attack

When Sarah had her first child nine months ago, she was elated. She and her husband, John, had waited ten years for this event, postponing their family until their careers were established. Yet Sarah was eager to give up her job as an account executive to be home with Emily.

The freshness of the situation began to wear off almost as quickly as the freshness of the diaper pail. Much to her horror, Sarah began to struggle with feelings of anger and bitterness toward not only Emily, but also John, who rarely helped with Emily's care. Sarah found herself resenting the fact that she and John never had any time alone at home anymore.

Although she loved Emily, Sarah grew impatient with her constant needs. She knew she should not be angry with Emily and felt guilty about her feelings most of the time. She wanted to be able to feel love for her baby and express that love.

"Today I will not feel angry with Emily," she would tell herself each morning. But before lunch, Sarah's anger would already be simmering. Although she coupled her determination with fervent prayers for strength and patience, Sarah found she was making no real changes in her feelings of anger and bitterness.

Sarah was using the method of direct attack: she was trying to pluck apples of anger and bitterness from her tree—only to find more growing in their places. Because emotions stem from thinking and behavior, Sarah cannot change her feelings without changing her thinking and behavior. Sarah cannot simply decide to feel a certain way and then wait for the feeling to follow.

Complicating the process of change is the interrelationship among feelings, thinking, and behavior. In Sarah's situation, her anger is influenced by her thinking (I think I deserve more freedom in my life; I think it is unfair that I am the only one to help out with Emily) and her behavior (staying home with Emily without any breaks). Her feelings of anger in turn influence her thinking and behavior, generating distorted thoughts (I may as well forget ever having my own time) and self-defeating behavior (refusing help from others). In addition, her thinking influences her behavior (I am upset so I have a right to slam my cupboard doors). Her behavior also influences her thinking (the more she slams, the angrier her thoughts become). Sarah is trapped in a vicious cycle of angry feelings, angry thoughts, and angry behavior. But to change her angry feelings, she must direct their energy toward her angry thoughts and behavior.

The Bible addresses our need to change both our thinking and our behavior. We are told in Romans 12:2 that we must renew our minds and learn to think with the mind of Christ. Commands concerning our behavior are plentiful: share with those in need and build up one another (Eph. 4:28–29) are two examples.

Problems arise when we limit change to only our behavior or only our thinking. The Pharisees of Jesus' time were guilty of the first: they changed their behavior but not their thinking. That is why Jesus said to them, "On the outside you appear to people as righteous but on the inside you are full of hypocrisy and wickedness" (Matt. 23:28). The result of changing behavior without changing thinking is legalism: the enforcement of rules becomes more important than the principles behind them. The outward appearance becomes the standard of judgment.

Another form of hypocrisy occurs when we change our thinking but not our behavior. We can see this in those who claim to be Christians and who use all the right words but fail to demonstrate a life of love. These are the folks who say, "I love you, neighbor," but then offer no help during times of need. Of them James says, "What good is it, my brothers, if a man claims to have faith but has no deeds? Faith by itself, if it is not accompanied by action, is dead" (James 2:14, 17). If a change in thinking is not accompanied by a change in behavior, then perhaps the thinking has never really changed. Most likely the lips say what the mind does not think and the heart does not feel.

When we want change to occur in the heart, we must work on both our thinking and our behavior. We must replace the wrong thinking with renewed thinking and the destructive behavior with Christ-like behavior; only then will the desired feelings follow.

Coping, Not Changing

Coping is what happens when people are unsuccessful in their attempts to change. Since they cannot get rid of their emotional pain, they find ways to reduce it. Coping helps them make it one day at a time; it is self-protective behavior. The two main coping styles are escape mechanisms and defense mechanisms.

Escape Mechanisms. When emotional pain becomes too great, some people seek to escape it through ways that make them forget, at least for awhile, their distress. The

34

method of escape can be as dangerous as drugs or as innocent as crossword puzzles. It can be anything that is carried to an excess. Too much sleeping, drinking, reading, shopping, or viewing of television can all be used for escape. This method hinders change because escape alleviates discomfort, reducing the need to work on the feelings. Of course, we all indulge in some escape mechanisms now and then; the peril lies in using them as our method of survival.

Defense Mechanisms. Defense mechanisms are widely used because they are so effective in making us feel better about ourselves. They help us shift responsibility for our thoughts, actions, and feelings. Unfortunately, you may not even be aware you are using them. As you read through this list, look for your favorite defenses. Until you can identify your coping styles, you will experience difficulty in carrying on the work of changing your feelings.

Rationalization—This defense mechanism works by allowing us to make up excuses or explanations for our source of pain. You have heard the phrase, "The devil made me do it"? With rationalization, a person says, "The devil (or someone or something) made me *feel* it." For example, a wife who experiences constant anger toward her husband might say, "My husband is a jerk. He makes me angry."

How often we use this defense: she makes me depressed, he makes me jealous, this or that makes me miserable. But regardless of what we think, no person or situation can force us to feel a certain way. We each define our own feelings based on our interpretation of events. If the accused person were actually responsible

35

for making us feel a certain way, everyone in our situation would feel the same way.

Our feelings are affected by our own attitudes, beliefs, intelligence, culture, and even gender. In fact, in the United States men more frequently describe themselves as angry, while women describe themselves as hurt or sad. Women turn their anger inside, making them twice as likely as men to become depressed. This gender difference has been confirmed in the laboratory, where reactions to provocation were studied. Despite having equivalent reactions in terms of heart rate and other physiological responses, men usually said they were angry while women said they were hurt or sad.[2]

We need to remember that even though people and circumstances may provoke us, they do not force us to feel a certain way. We choose to become angry or sad. We need to recognize our typical emotional responses before we can change them. If you always respond with anger to your spouse's criticisms, you need to be aware of this pattern. Once you are able to take responsibility for your reactions, you can begin to explore the source of your anger. If you identify with the woman who says her husband makes her angry, you need to look at your attitudes toward your spouse, your beliefs about why he is demeaning you, and your response to his criticisms.

Intellectualization—The intellectualizer attempts to avoid his emotions through the use of reason and logic. He may be able to offer an impressive description of his attitudes and motivations, but he lacks an awareness of his feelings. You have met intellectualizers— they are the folks who quote self-help psychology books and seem to have a thorough understanding of themselves. But they don't.

Displacement—This defense mechanism could

also be called "abusing the innocent." The most commonly cited example is the man who comes home after a hard day at the office and kicks the dog. He is angry with his boss but doesn't feel he can express his anger directly, so he displaces his feelings on the dog. Although you may never kick a pet, do you yell at your kids when you are upset about something else? Or talk sharply with your spouse because you are anxious about your job? Displacement is a malevolent expression of emotional energy because it hurts someone else.

Denial—Because many of us grew up believing negative feelings are sinful, we often deny having them. We refuse to even acknowledge the feeling, pushing it inside. Instead we concentrate on happy thoughts, forcing ourselves to engage in positive thinking.

A young woman is dropped by her boyfriend, but instead of working through her feelings of sadness and anger, she denies them: "There are other fish in the sea. I'm sure I'll find a better catch." She feels the hurt, but she doesn't want to deal with it. Even though she thinks she has buried her feelings, they will resurface in later relationships, probably with renewed intensity. Looking on the bright side is a healthy response only when the dark side is acknowledged.

Repression—Repression is denial pushed to the extreme. Not only are the feelings pushed inside, but so is the memory of the event that caused the pain. Because the distress was too horrendous to handle, it all had to be "forgotten." Repression may be a child's response to molestation or an adult's response to emotional trauma. But even though the event and feelings that accompanied it seem to be safely tucked away, they create a vague sense of anxiety and discomfort: "I'm unhappy, but I don't know why." Certain places and

37

faces may trigger increased anxiety, and until the memory is dealt with, the distress will remain.

Projection—Projection is another form of denial. We deny having certain feelings and instead accuse someone else of having them. A husband is angry with his wife, but he asks why she is angry with him. He does not want to face his anger, so he projects it onto his wife, who may be bewildered by his accusations.

Reaction Formation—This defense mechanism occurs when someone feels a negative emotion, yet behaves as if she feels the exact opposite way. For example, a mother is envious of her daughter because of her beauty. Instead of acting envious, however, she overwhelms her daughter with compliments while degrading herself. Or a wife who feels disgust for her husband tells everyone how wonderful he is. People engage in reaction formation because they cannot bear to acknowledge their true feelings. Until they do, they have no hope of changing them.

Escape and defense mechanisms are protective behaviors—ways to respond to keep us from ever looking at how we really feel. Although we feel better when we use these mechanisms, an excessive reliance upon them can do more harm than good. Like the caged bird with clipped wings, we are safe, but constricted and confined. In our protected environment we fail to realize we were designed for something better. Our Creator made us to depend upon him, not on our own protective devices. Until we can shift from self-defense to God-dependence, we will always miss the power available to us, the promise that we can "soar on wings like eagles [and] run and not grow weary" (Isa. 40:31).

Disciplined Grace: The Foundation for Real Change

Suppose you had been ill for a long time. At the time when you could almost smell death, a stranger appeared with a potion that would restore your health. He would not sell you any—he said it cost more than you could pay—but he was eager to give you all you needed. In order for it to be effective, however, he said you had to move to the mountains on the other side of the world. After thinking over his offer, you decided to accept the stranger's potion and promptly relocated to the mountains. You were delighted to find that the stranger had told you the truth; you were indeed healthy.

What was responsible for the change in you? It certainly was not living in the mountains. What cured you was the stranger's potion. Yet living in the mountains was also necessary. Using this allegory, we can begin to understand how real change occurs in us. First of all, it is God who changes us at the deepest level of our being. Romans 5:17 tells us that righteousness is a gift from God; it is a gift that comes through Jesus Christ when we make him Savior and Lord of our lives (Phil. 1:11). But we also discover in Hebrews 12:11 that righteousness is produced by discipline. How do we reconcile this apparent difference?

Looking again at the allegory, you can see that the mountains did not cure you; they were simply the proper place for the potion to work. In the same way, disciplining ourselves in the ways instructed by God does not make us healthy, but it puts us where God can work in us. When we discipline ourselves to put God's kingdom first in our lives (Matt. 6:33), we enable God to make changes in us. It is not the prayer, worship, Bible study, Scripture memorization, fasting, or Christian service that change us. But these spiritual disciplines make us changeable—so that God can do the required work.

The fact that God changes us is *grace;* we have done nothing to deserve his generosity. But this change also requires something of us—*discipline*—which allows God to work in us. Richard Foster termed this process *disciplined grace*. We encourage you to read his book *Celebration of Discipline*, in which he shares insights on how twelve different disciplines can help us toward inner transformation.[3]

As we become transformed, we encounter more of the living God and his many gifts for us. Three of his gifts are vital for emotional change and are the same three that counselors attempt to emulate, albeit in their limited ways. These gifts are insight, security, and strength.

Insight. God can give us insight into ourselves because he knows us. He made us. He knows our past, our present, and our future. And he offers to share his knowledge with us so we may know and understand ourselves. "Search me, O God, and know my heart," prayed David in Psalm 139:23. While a skilled counselor may offer insights into our thinking, feeling, and behavior, he or she cannot peer into our souls. God's knowledge of us, however, knows no bounds.

Security. As we grow in our relationship with God, we discover just how much he loves us. Because this perfect love drives out fear (1 John 4:18), we become freed from our fear of change. Change, after all, is a scary proposition. Even when we are miserable, at least we know what to expect! Because the prospect of change brings with it uncertainty, we must become convinced that God is working for our good. In a similar manner, a counselor must win our trust before he or she can begin working with us.

Strength. Have you ever felt too distressed to pray? Or felt too discouraged to read the Bible? What happens to our inner transformation when we fail to maintain spiritual discipline? That is the time when we can be thankful that it is God doing the work instead of us. We can draw on God's strength; we can rest in his power. God understands our weaknesses. His power is made perfect in them (2 Cor. 12:9). It is he alone who restores our souls and empowers us to draw close to him.

In a similar way, counselors try to give support to their clients. When clients are ready to give up hope, counselors provide it for them. Studies have shown that counselors' expectations for their clients have a relatively greater impact than counselees' expectations. God has great expectations for his children. He promises to carry on his work in us "to completion" (Phil. 1:6). We all need to borrow strength at one time or another, so we can take joy in the fact that God is the strength of our hearts (Ps. 73:26).

Yet we cannot wait for God to shower us with these gifts. We must move to the mountains where the renewing rains come regularly. Once there, we need to remember that the mountains are not always an easy place to live. They are steep, have deep valleys, and are dark in places. Many times we will not feel God's presence there. But the mountains are where God lives and works, and he promises to work changes in us, if we choose to live there with him.

41

FOUR

Seeing Red for Right and Wrong Reasons—Anger

Lisa and her husband, Rob, were new Christians at their church. In their forties, they appeared happily married—until Rob left Lisa for another woman. Although devastated, Lisa never showed any sign of anger, not even when Rob started bringing his girlfriend to their church (even before he filed for divorce). Instead Lisa blamed herself for her failings as a wife, developed stomach problems, and quietly quit going to church.

Sam and Lorraine were another couple in the same church. Their five children lived in terror of Sam's verbal, and frequently physical, abuse. Although Lorraine witnessed the abuse, she was too intimidated by her husband to stop it. Because Sam was an elder in the church and well-respected, Lorraine never expressed her anger to anyone. Instead she simply prayed for her children.

Obviously, anger should have been the response in both of these situations. Lisa was justified to feel anger at her husband, who betrayed their marriage vows, and at her church, which neglected to even suggest to Rob that his actions were wrong. And Lorraine's failure to express anger allowed her husband's abuse to continue. (Of course, her husband's abusive behavior represents inappropriate expression of anger on his part as well.)

Lisa and Lorraine are not alone in their mishandling of anger. Anger is one of the least understood emotions, possibly because many of us have been taught from childhood that anger is a sin. By itself, however, anger is never a wrong reaction, and it is a correct response when we become angry for the right reasons. In this chapter we will look at the two sides of anger—righteous and not-so-righteous—and the appropriate handling of each.

RIGHTEOUS ANGER

Of the several hundred times that anger is mentioned in the Bible, more than eighty percent concern God's anger. Some of the descriptions of God's anger should chill our bones, such as this passage: "Now leave me alone so that my anger may burn against them and that I may destroy them" (Ex. 32:10).

What made God so angry that he wanted to destroy the people he loved? Sin. God is both good and just, so he cannot tolerate evil. To allow his people to live in sin would fail to be an act of love because with sin comes hurt and a violation of good. God's anger at wrongdoing is necessary because of his goodness and love for us.

Evil should also evoke anger in us. Without anger, we have no energy to right the wrongs of this world. Martin Luther said, "When I am angry, I preach well and pray better."[1] If Lisa had allowed herself to experience anger, she might have saved her marriage, her stomach, or both. And if Lorraine had recognized

43

and expressed her anger in appropriate channels, her children might have been spared their anguish. As Melvin E. Wheatley, Jr., noted, "There are situations in life in which the absence of anger would be the essence of evil."[2]

We also need to examine the things that make us mad. Because emotions are based in our investments, our anger helps us to see what is important to us. We get angry in proportion to the value of something to us. That is why we can get so furious with a loved one—we have a great deal of ourselves invested in the relationship. Conversely, when someone or something fails to arouse our ire, we need to realize our lack of investment.

Which makes you more angry: That your neighbor neglects to mow her lawn or that she neglects her children? That your neighborhood raises your taxes or that it encourages prejudice against minorities? How often we fail to feel anger against evil until it touches our own lives! Someone once said that the size of a man can be known by the size of the things that make him mad. We need to continually ask ourselves, "Does what angers God also anger me?" God calls us to get good and angry at injustices.

NOT-SO-RIGHTEOUS ANGER

Even when we fail to get angry at evil done to others, we usually have no trouble feeling wrath toward those who wrong us. Like Lisa and Lorraine, many times we are entitled to be angry. When God's standards are violated, we should be so angry that we want to correct the injustice.

Yet most of us would agree that we often become angry over matters that do not concern God's righteousness. As a Scottish hymnist and preacher put it, "There are times when I do well to be angry, but I mistake the times."[3] We find ourselves in an emotional whirlwind over the smallest slight. What causes our anger in these situations?

Unrealistic Expectations

Anger is directly related to our goals and expectations. When these expectations are not met, we become angry. If your expectations are high, you will experience more anger and frustration than someone whose desires and goals are more modest. If you have no expectations, you will experience no anger.[4]

If you desire and expect a beautiful home, well-behaved children, money in the bank, a fulfilling career, thoughtful friends, a romantic spouse, and good health, you will contend with anger whenever these desires are blocked. If instead you don't expect the world to treat you perfectly, you will be angry less frequently.

Anger is a common response among toddlers, who expect to be able to do physical tasks beyond their ability. When our daughter was two years old, she experienced tantrums stemming from her inability to smooth her doll's blanket perfectly. Had she not cared how wrinkled the quilt was, she could have played happily. Instead she often threw down her doll and refused to play at all. Unfortunately, some of us never get beyond the toddler stage and stay angry all of our lives over things we cannot control.

Expectations get in the way of gratitude. When we believe we deserve something good, we are less likely to feel grateful for it when we get it. And when we fail to receive what we think we deserve, we feel cheated. Yet we live in an imperfect world where many desires go unfulfilled. Jesus warned against putting expectations on other people, saying that even when we do good, we should not expect anything in return (Luke 6:35).

If we expect our spouse to make us happy, we will be angry whenever he is tired or thoughtless. If we expect our job to bring fulfillment, we will be angry when we are passed by for a promotion. If we expect our friends to make us feel important, we will be angry whenever they slight us. If we expect God to give us a perfect life, we will be angry when we experience trials. And if we expect that we should never make mistakes, we will be angry every time we are less than perfect.

What, then, can we expect? The Bible tells us that in this world we can expect to have troubles. Our friends will betray us, our careers will frustrate us, our family will disappoint us, our children will rebel against us, our treasures will rust, and we will fall short of our own ambitions. Yet we can expect that God will be with us as we pass through difficulties. We can remember that through it all, God is there, weeping with us.

Misplaced Expectations

Knowing that we will endure problems in this life should not make us pessimists, however. Our culture has a skewed concept of suffering that maintains it is to be avoided. In contrast, the apostle Paul suggested that suffering should be a cause for joy because it brings about perseverance, character, and hope. We can always put our expectations in hope, he wrote, because it is based in God's love and will never disappoint us (Rom. 5:4–5).

We can be confident that one future day we will

realize the glory to which we have been called. We will know the fulfillment of our expectations as we become what God intended us to be before the Fall. In the meantime, we have to learn to subdue our expectations for perfection in this life and place them on our future glory.

Learning to be content with less in this life is difficult if we look to this life to meet our expectations. We can reroute our expectations only as we see past the temporary nature of this life into the eternity that follows. This heavenly vision need not make us believe there is no earthly good, however. It simply helps us to remember that we were not placed on this planet to fulfill our needs but instead to glorify God through the love we pour upon others. If we focus on loving others and meeting their needs, and if we keep our own expectations of love dependent upon God, then we will truly experience life as God intended it.

Projected Expectations

When we fix unrealistic and misplaced expectations on others, they can become angry, too. If our family and friends believe they can never meet our expectations, they will feel terrible frustration.

Recently a Midwest community was shocked with the news of the suicide of a "perfect" teenager. He was class valedictorian, excelled in athletics, and was well-respected by both adults and kids. Yet after graduation he entered psychiatric treatment for depression, brought on by the pressure he said he felt to live up to his father's expectations. Even though this boy had become "the best" at whatever he tried, he believed it still was not good enough to please his demanding father. After his suicide, the boy's friends remarked that they had never seen him angry. Instead he had turned his anger upon himself.

When projected expectations don't bring about consequences as tragic as this, they still create problems, especially for our families. They are one of the prime causes of childhood depression, teenage rebellion, and broken relationships. Whenever we set a standard and say, "Meet this or I can't love you," we set the stage for sorrow.

EXPRESSING OUR ANGER

Anger is said to be the first emotion that we experience, yet the last feeling we learn how to handle. Infants as young as four months of age experience recognizable anger that can be differentiated from vague feelings of distress. It is not our feelings of anger that pose the problem, however; it is how we handle our angry feelings. "In your anger do not sin," Paul wrote (Eph. 4:26). Note that Paul did not call anger itself a sin, nor did he advise the Ephesians not to express their anger. Instead he cautioned that anger should be handled without inflicting hurt upon others or ourselves. To handle anger in this manner, we need to look at four areas: recognizing our anger, rooting it out, channeling it, and communicating it.

Recognizing Anger

"I am angry nearly every day of my life, Jo; but I have learned not to show it; and I still hope to learn not to feel it, though it may take me another forty years to do so."

When Marmee uttered those words to Jo in *Little Women*,[5] she was speaking on behalf of many Christians and many women. The idea that women in general and Christians in particular should deny their anger has been passed from generation to generation. Mary Ellen Ashcroft, author of *Temptations Women Face*, wrote that women are taught from childhood not to fight or get angry.[6] Researcher N. K. Hayles observed that it is a "necessity [of women] to deny and disguise [their] anger."[7]

Unfortunately, denial does not rid one of anger; the feelings simply emerge in another form. In fact, one psychiatrist, Teresa Bernardez-Bonesatti, speculates that women's anger and their attempts to deny it are responsible for most of the dysfunctional behaviors that trouble women today.[8]

Anger has been described as an acid that can do more harm to the vessel in which it is stored than to anything on which it is poured. This idea has been studied since the 1950s, when scientists began exploring a link between Type A behavior (hostile emotions and driving ambition) and heart disease. Recent research has shown, however, that hostility—not driving ambition—is connected with heart disease.

When we are angry, our bodies respond with increased levels of certain hormones that adversely affect the cardiovascular system. Redford Williams cites numerous studies showing that people who experience these large and frequent increases in body chemicals are at greater risk for heart disease.[9]

An important point to note is that even if we don't recognize our angry feelings, our bodies experience the biochemical changes—and the resulting physical damage. The first step toward controlling hostility, then, is to know when it is there.

Women especially have a difficult time admitting their anger. Research shows that when equally provoked, men say they are angry and women describe themselves as sad or depressed.[10] Psychologist Harriet Lerner noted that male patients typically say, "I was angry," while female patients say, "I was hurt." She wrote:

> This phrase, "I was hurt," is a telling one. For when a legitimate anger cannot be acknowledged, recognized and expressed, women do, indeed, "hurt." Their hurt may take the form of headaches, fatigue, depression, or sexual disinterest. Or it may even express itself in intellectual dullness or a lack of interest or capacity for creative and original work.[11]

We may repress and deny our anger for so long that we honestly cannot recognize it. Discovering it, then, involves not looking for things that make us mad, but trying to determine what things make us feel hurt or depressed. One way to do this is to keep a pocket notebook handy throughout the day and write down situations and conversations that bring about sad feelings or hostile thoughts. This may require some effort, but the notes will help us discover patterns in our emotional reactions and will sharpen our ability to recognize anger.

We also must examine how we treat our bodies. "Angry people do angry things to themselves," warned Dr. Ernest H. Johnson in *The Deadly Emotions*. "They smoke, they drink, they do drugs; they slowly do things to destroy themselves."[12]

Until we are willing to recognize and admit our anger, we cannot move on to the next step.

Rooting Out Anger

Because anger is a reaction to the frustration of our expectations and goals, it can tell a lot about us. "Tell me what ticks you off, and I will tell you what makes you tick," wrote Lloyd J. Ogilvie.[13]

When we become angry, we need to examine why we are angry. What expectation or goal has been blocked? Is it a realistic or unrealistic goal? Who or what is keeping us from attaining the goal? Whom or what do we hold responsible for keeping us from our desires?

Sally came in for marital counseling six months after the birth of her third son. She said she had not been able to shake her postpartum blues, and she was concerned that she had no interest in her children, her husband, or her church. Her husband, a nice, well-meaning fellow, could not understand her difficulties because his job provided the family with considerable material security.

Within a few counseling sessions, however, Sally's underlying anger began to surface. She revealed that she had always wanted to complete college and pursue a professional career and that she perceived the birth of each child as yet another obstacle to her goals and desires. She also harbored resentment toward her husband, whom she perceived as "forcing" her into the homemaker role.

Her husband was surprised to hear Sally talk this way; indeed, Sally herself was surprised. She had buried her anger so deeply that she was unaware of it. The process of blunting her anger had resulted in a blunting of her other feelings as well, resulting in her general lack of interest in life. Recognizing her anger and discovering its root was Sally's first step toward recovering her feelings.

Sometimes when we search for the source of our anger, we find God at the other end. Even then we may hesitate to actually call our feelings "anger." We may think "if only" thoughts such as, "If only God had intervened, my son would still be alive," or "If only God had shown me what a jerk he was, I would never have married him." We stop short of confronting God with our anger, however, perhaps because we believe it is a sin to be angry toward God. The good news is that God can tolerate our anger—indeed, he already knows the thoughts and feelings we try to bury inside us.

Whether we find God, another person, or even ourselves at the root of our anger, we need to recognize the damage that blame can inflict. As long as we blame others, we give them control over our lives, which in turn causes more anger. When we blame ourselves, our anger can turn inward to create depression. Blame will keep us from ever dealing effectively with our anger.

Once we have identified the source of our anger, the next step is to forgive—another person, God, or ourselves. Forgiveness is what philosopher Hannah Arendt called "the only power that can stop the inexorable stream of painful memories."[14] With forgiving must also come forgetting, which means we must choose not to let our memories control us.

If we cannot identify the root of our anger on our own or with the help of friends, it is time to seek professional help. Unresolved anger will destroy the joy in life.

Channeling Anger

Because anger is energy, it must be channeled into something or it continues to build up and inflict damage inside our bodies. Anger causes distress because it is a signal that we need to take action.

In trying to provide a healthy channel for hostility and aggression, some counselors suggest therapy that involves punching soft objects, screaming, or throwing tantrums in a padded room. While this clearly makes use of angry energy, recent research shows that it does nothing to abate it. Becoming physically aggressive can actually increase the level of hostility and the need to vent more anger.

Less hostile physical activities are more effective at diminishing anger's energy. Try a brisk walk, energetic housecleaning, or vigorous exercises. All will serve to cool anger's hot feelings. And while we sometimes need to put off our anger until we cool off, we still have to deal with it. Putting off anger is not a replacement for dealing with it. We can more effectively handle our anger, however, when we have released some of its steam.

A constructive channel for anger is to use the energy of the emotion to confront wrongdoing or correct an injustice. Lisa and Lorraine, who were introduced at the beginning of this chapter, could have used their angry energy to bring about change in their situations.

We must be cautious that our zeal for justice doesn't cause us to inflict further hurt, however. We knew a young woman who was so angry at being neglected by her mother that she determined to have a daughter and give her the attention she herself had lacked. Unfortunately, she bore two sons before having a girl. In her quest to right her mother's wrong, this woman repeated her mother's sin of neglect in the life of her boys. We must remember that our first calling is not to deliver justice, but to live God's love.

The apostle Paul suggested this very love as another constructive channel for anger in his letter to the Roman church. When others wrong us, we are to perform acts of love for them, he wrote in Romans 12:20–21, thus overcoming evil with good. He warned that when we fail to love our enemies, we risk being overcome by their evil.

At first glance, this may seem to smack of hypocrisy. Why should we act loving toward someone we don't love? It is not hypocritical love, however, because we acknowledge our angry feelings. We simply choose to love. This concept is reflected in the therapy technique of behavior modification, which focuses on changing behavior first and waiting for the feelings to follow.

To love one who has stirred angry feelings in us requires a change in our appraisal—the way we interpret that person's actions. We often make others into bad guys because we ascribe inaccurate motives to their actions. A friend doesn't call, so we infer that she doesn't care. In reality, she was too depressed to pick up the phone. A husband goes overboard with unsolicited advice, and we believe he thinks we are too dumb to make our own decisions. Actually, he derives his own sense of value from trying to advise others.

Because we can lack awareness of our own motives, we should never assume to know why another person acts in a particular way. Instead we must remember that we are all broken and wounded people acting out of our hurts and needs. When we see those who have hurt us as hurting also, we take the first step toward being able to love as God loves.

Communicating Anger

The English language has a large number of words to describe anger, ranging from annoyance to wrath. Despite the expansive vocabulary available to us, however, we often have trouble saying what we mean when communicating our anger. Too often we end up expressing ourselves by one of the following destructive styles.

Blow Up. This "big bang" is the cursing, screaming, and stomping that often accompany anger. Although this type of ventilation might seem to offer an immediate release for anger, it actually serves to increase our hostility. It also stimulates anger in those who are the recipient of the outburst. Because it's tough to let our light shine when our fuse has blown, we need to take our anger for a walk while we cool off.

Clam up. This style involves keeping our anger inside and pretending that everything is fine, particularly when we are angry at someone we perceive as powerful. Even when confronted, we don't allow anyone to pry open our angry feelings.

Clamming up is just as unhealthy as blowing up because even though we fail to express our anger to others, we usually rehearse it over and over in our mind. We may go over situations and conversations, often adding dialogue that never occurred. "I know that if I had said ... he would have said ...," and "I bet he thought ..." Every rehearsal kindles the fire of the original angry feelings. Every new slight is added to the record of earlier wrongs.

Clamming up works like a trash compactor: it stuffs and smashes angry feelings into a dense weight that is greater than anyone can bear. One feeling is pushed onto another, until they all become so jumbled that we may feel angry all the time. We need to take out the "garbage" every day, no matter how smelly, and not allow "the sun [to] go down while [we] are still angry" (Eph. 4:26).

When clamming up, we also reveal our anger in passive-aggressive behavior, such as forgetfulness, tardiness, procrastination, or carelessness, all exercised with a smile and an apology. While outwardly "happy as a clam," we may "forget" to meet someone with whom we are angry or we may show up late. We may not even realize that we are trying to punish those who have stirred our anger.

Shut up. When we "shut up," we are obviously angry, but we refuse to talk about our anger. We express our anger by communicating it nonverbally. We know of a woman who once became so incensed at her family that she stopped talking to her husband and children for four weeks. Even though her anger was not verbalized, it was actively and clearly expressed through body language: the cold shoulder, crossed arms, upturned nose, and wicked stares. This silent treatment is deadly because it effectively terminates any chance to work through a problem.

Show Up. Sometimes when we are angry, we try to make someone else look bad, which makes us think we

look good. So we resort to sarcasm. We say the most hurtful thing we can think of, and then add, "Of course, I'm only kidding. Can't you take a joke?" The next time you are tempted to be sarcastic, remember the literal meaning of this verbal weapon is "to tear flesh." Sarcasm is simply criticism packaged in humor. When you unwrap the joke, you find hostility at its center.

Throw up. Perhaps the most common way we communicate our anger is to "throw up" all the past ways another has hurt us. Instead of focusing on the immediate hurt, we dig up all the other angry feelings against the offender that we can muster. Thus a disagreement between a husband and wife about finances escalates into an all-out war with every past grievance thrown into the battle. "Throw up" is often used with "blow up," as tempers get out of control and respect disappears. If you frequently use this style, you need to examine what is keeping your past in the present and deal with it once and for all.

Tear up. Sometimes the most important thing about fighting becomes winning, having the last word. We may try to intimidate others through an explosive temper or threats of violence, or we may withhold affection. We may use persistent and insistent words to convince our "opponent" of our viewpoint. Keep in mind, however, that the word *convince* comes from a Latin word meaning "to conquer." When anger brings about a battleground, no one is the winner. Not only do we tear up individuals, but we also tear up relationships.

Seeing Red, Feeling Blue, or in the Pink

Communicating Anger Constructively

Breaking out of these destructive styles and communicating anger effectively is not easy. It requires a four-way change: in authenticity, aim, attitude, and appraisal.

Authenticity. Before we can effectively communicate our anger to others, we have to be willing to be honest in our relationships. This is difficult because honesty involves the risk that the person we confront might end the relationship rather than work through it. So we often settle for "safe," superficial affiliations that demand little of us. We tend to avoid conflict, even when that conflict would bring about a deeper, more meaningful relationship.

Yet the human personality has a built-in inclination to reveal itself, psychologist Sidney Jourard suggested. Jourard, who studied self-disclosure, wrote in his book *The Transparent Self* that withdrawal leads to the disintegration of the personality while honesty can prevent both mental and physical illness.[15] Authenticity not only builds our relationships, but it also strengthens us as individuals.

Aim. Once we are willing to be honest with ourselves, others, and God, anger can be used as a tool to help us build relationships. Our anger can become a "positive motivator to be used in giving one another feedback about how life can be lived more productively," suggested Les Carter in his book *Good 'n' Angry*.[16]

If our aim in communicating anger is to build relationships and minister to others, we will not simply ventilate our angry feelings or try to drive others into

submission. Understanding will become more important than winning, and gentle assertion will replace aggression.

This type of constructive communication calls for more listening than talking. The goal is not just to be heard, but to hear. One important tool to use is reflective listening, where we repeat, in our own words, what we think the other person is saying. By using gentle touching and expressions of affection (even when we don't feel like it), we will help bring about an atmosphere conducive to understanding. It's also essential that we balance our criticism with encouraging words to defuse the level of hurt and anger.

Statements of feelings instead of accusatory words also help to promote understanding. Rather than saying, "You never come home on time," try, "I *feel* lonely when you're not home by 6:00 P.M." Ask questions that foster openness instead of defensiveness. Ask, "Do you miss me, too?" instead of, "Do you stay late at work to avoid spending time with me?" Before we speak, it's good to remember the Bible's instruction that our words should be "only what is helpful for building others up" (Eph. 4:29).

Keeping our voice volume low helps as well. "A gentle answer turns away wrath," wrote King Solomon, "but a harsh word stirs up anger" (Prov. 15:1). Our gentle voice will not only calm those listening, but it will also quiet our own spirit. When voices rise, it's time to retreat until tempers cool.

Attitude. "There can be no friendship where there is no freedom," wrote William Penn in *Some Fruits of Solitude*. "Friendship loves a free air, and will not be fenced up in straight and narrow enclosures."[17] We need to give our friends—and relatives—freedom to be themselves and to do things that anger us, even if we think we could improve their lives (if only they would listen to us!). The key to allowing others this freedom is to remember that we are not responsible for them. We may be responsible *to* them—to care for them, honor them, love them—but we are not responsible *for* anyone's actions but our own.

We approach others with an improper attitude when we expect them to behave the way we think is best. When trying to communicate our anger, we need to replace an *expectful* attitude with a *respectful* attitude, or we will simply stoke the fire.

When we want to express our anger effectively, we should leave behind our high horses and upturned noses. We need the same attitude as Jesus, who "made himself nothing, taking the very nature of a servant" (Phil. 2:7). It is this servant attitude that forms the basis for building any relationship.

Even when we have no respect for what a person has done or said, we can demonstrate this humble attitude. The Bible teaches us that we honor others not for what they have done, but for who they are—people made in the image of God. Respecting others, even when we are angry with them, is simply granting them the worth already given them by God.

Appraisal. We need to decide what is worth our anger. Sometimes a casual remark that rubs us the wrong way is best left alone. When we feel hurt or angry, we need to ask, "What would be gained if I confronted this person?" Sometimes we need to let actions and remarks slide off us, particularly when they are not intended to hurt us or when they are delivered by someone who is not interested in building a good relationship with us.

Perhaps you have a relative who loves to sling arrows of sarcasm your way, with little interest in how you are affected. You can learn to keep this person from penetrating your emotions if you reappraise the situation and decide it is not worth your anger. Instead you can choose to allow your relative the freedom to be a jerk. You need to remind yourself that you do not deserve those arrows of sarcasm, that you are not responsible for the arrows, and that you can choose to let them simply fall to the ground.

Unfortunately, we often encounter people in our lives who refuse to hear our concerns and who block all attempts to build a better relationship. Because we cannot take responsibility for another person's actions and attitudes, we need not feel responsible if our attempts at constructive communication fail. We can keep the door open, but we shouldn't try to drag someone through it. At times like that, it's important to focus on building up other healthy relationships.

FIVE
Feeling Blue When We Experience Loss—Sadness

Loss can cause great sadness and stress in our lives because we lose a bit of ourselves each time we part with something important to us.[1] Whether we lose a loved one, our health, our freedom, or our job, each loss brings about a change in who we are and a resulting feeling of sadness.

Although painful to experience, sadness is actually a positive response to loss. Unfortunately, we rarely feel just sadness when we suffer loss. Negative emotions (such as anger, anxiety, guilt, envy, and shame) taint our sad feelings and disrupt the process of grieving. In fact, for sadness to remain our primary emotion, three conditions must be met: (1) we must accept the loss as irrevocable, (2) we must attribute no blame, and (3) we must have hope for the future.[2] Unless all three conditions are present, the process of grieving is lengthened and made more difficult.

Good grieving, then, is grief that has those three conditions as its foundation. We have a powerful example of it in the Bible's account of how King David dealt with the death of his infant son. Because of David's adultery with Bathsheba and his role in her husband's death (2 Sam. 11), God told David that the son of his union with Bathsheba would die. When the child became ill, David fasted and prayed for seven days, pleading with God to spare his child. Upon the boy's death, however, David "got up from the ground . . . washed, put on lotions . . . changed his clothes . . . [and] went into the house of the Lord and worshiped" (2 Sam. 12:20).

The Bible says that David's servants were baffled by the change in his behavior. Why was David no longer stricken with immobilizing grief? The answer is that David accepted his loss as irrevocable, he blamed no one, and he put his hope in the future.

"Now that [my child] is dead, why should I fast? Can I bring him back again?" David asked (2 Sam. 12:23). David entertained no notion that God would restore his son's life. He accepted his son's death as final.

Neither did David blame others for the loss. He did not try to accuse Bathsheba of enticing him, nor did he hold God ultimately responsible. Instead he admitted his sin and accepted God's forgiveness (Ps. 51).

Most importantly, David had hope for the future. He looked forward to being reunited with his son after his earthly life, proclaiming, "I will go to him, but he will not return to me" (2 Sam. 12:23). He also showed his hope for his present life when he "comforted his wife Bathsheba, and he went to her and lay with her. She gave birth to a son, and they named him Solomon" (2 Sam. 12:24). Even though David knew he would face more trouble in this life as a result of his sin, he did not lose hope. His hope for the future resulted in the birth of Solomon, the wisest man ever to live.

WORKING THROUGH LOSS

Grieving is an intensely personal experience, and no rules or steps can whisk us painlessly through the process. It is exhausting and unpredictable work, fraught with pitfalls and relapses. We can make a deliberate decision, however, to fight against the negative emotions that interfere with sadness. Whether our loss concerns our loved ones, possessions, career, reputation, values, or dreams, we can make choices that help us accept our loss, attribute no blame, and hope for the future. But we must be willing to work through the loss, instead of allowing ourselves to be victimized by it.

Accepting Loss

Acceptance of loss is not easy. Our first response is usually denial: "No, it can't be true. I won't let it be true." Until we come to terms with our loss, however, we will not experience sadness, which is a necessary step toward healing. As long as we struggle to hold onto what is no longer ours, we will experience emotions such as anger, anxiety, and envy. We must view our loss as irrevocable so that feelings of sadness can occur.

When wishful thinking asserts itself, we must actively push the thoughts away and speak the truth, perhaps out loud: "My divorce is final . . . my job is over . . . my child is dead." We can't waste our time and emotions thinking about how happy we could be *if only* our loss were restored. Holding onto fantastical thoughts is a luxury we cannot afford. Life as we knew it is over, and it will never again be the same. Although nothing can take away our memories, we must cherish them without trying to make them part of our present.

Feeling Blue When We Experience Loss—Sadness

In order to face up to the reality of the loss, we cannot keep living as if nothing has changed. If we lose our job, we cannot spend money as if we had a paycheck. If our child has died, we cannot keep her bedroom intact, ready for her to return.

Accepting death is most difficult when we have no finality of the loss. Those whose loved ones are listed as missing in action from past wars may continue to deny the possibility of death even decades later. When the bodies of drowning or accident victims are never recovered, families may continue to fantasize about the return of their loved ones.

Funerals are in fact a necessary part of healing for the survivors because they make us deal with the irreversibility of death. While viewing the lifeless body of a loved one is heart-wrenching, it imparts finality to our loss.

Another necessary step in accepting a loss is to restructure and reschedule life. A woman who dined out every Tuesday night with her spouse before his death might use that night to volunteer at a homeless shelter, hospital, or children's home. By doing so, she would find living people who needed her.

Part of restructuring life can mean that we revise our daily schedule. Shop at different stores. Make new friends. Discover untapped talents. Because too much change can be overwhelming, however, we shouldn't try to alter our entire life in one month. Rather we must make adjustments in small steps.

Attributing No Blame

Our suffering will be prolonged if we blame others or ourselves for our loss. Instead of focusing on our loss, we dwell on the person or action we hold responsible for the harm. As long as we blame others, we give them control over us. This brings about feelings of anger and bitterness instead of sadness. When we blame ourselves, our anger can turn inward to create depression.

Hoping for the Future

Hope is what keeps sadness from turning into depression. In depression, we generalize our loss to our whole life. We see an empty and barren future and question why we should continue living. If we lose a job, for instance, we believe that our life will forever be devoid of meaning. Sad feelings remain untainted by depression only when we believe that life can be good again, that we have a purpose yet to fulfill, that the future promises hope.

Some researchers believe that one reason our generation is experiencing record rates of depression is our lack of hope for the future.[3] Given the economic and social problems of the United States (and many other countries), faith in the future seems fragile at best. As Christians, however, we have a definite advantage in our ability to hope because our hope need not be based on an employer's whim or the rate of inflation. Our hope is built on a loving God who knows our needs.

In the midst of loss, however, it can be easy to forget about God, as did Martin Luther once when he was despondent. One day he was surprised to see his wife dressed in mourning. When he asked her who had died, she responded, "God in his heaven is dead."

"How can you talk such nonsense, Katie? How can God die? Why, he is immortal and will live through all eternity. How can you doubt it?" he admonished her. As

Luther listened to his own words, he began to regain his hope and master his depression.[4]

Reflecting on God and his unfailing love for us is one step toward bringing back hope. "We wait in hope for the Lord; he is our help and our shield," wrote David in Psalm 33:20. The Psalms hold comforting words for those who are grieving.

Another way to generate hope is to drink in the beauty of God's creation. Author Mary Jane Worden, who lost her husband in a car accident, suggested that our God-given capacity to appreciate beauty helps in our recovery from loss. "Beauty can help to bring healing—rainbows, mountains, woolly lambs, fresh strawberries on homemade ice cream, the crisp clean feel of sun-dried sheets. These places and things were somehow soothing to my soul," she wrote.[5]

To renew our hope, we also must make ourselves reenter the world. Although we often seek isolation when we experience loss, at some point we have to involve ourselves again with life on this earth. As we take part in activities and in other people's lives, we begin to rediscover fulfillment and purpose. As we make new commitments, we reposition ourselves to benefit from gains that generate hope.

TURNING LOSS INTO GAIN

With loss comes the question, Why? Why does God allow suffering? Why do bad things happen to good people? How do we reconcile evil and suffering with an omnipotent and good God?

When our friends discovered that their three-year-old daughter had been sexually abused by a relative, they requested our immediate presence. When we arrived at their home, we found open Bibles lying throughout the room and the mother rocking herself on the floor, with the huge family Bible in her lap. "I've looked in all our Bibles, and I can't find the reason why this happened to our baby," she cried. In her grief, the mother had reasoned that if the answer was not in one of the small Bibles, then it would be in the biggest one they had.

Why the innocent suffer, however, is never directly addressed in the Bible. Even Job, who lost his children, possessions, and health, was never told the reasons for his travail. He never knew of the cosmic contest initiated by Satan to test his allegiance to God. Instead Job was admonished by God simply to trust in his sovereignty.

We can be sure, however, that we do not suffer without reason, even though God shrouds its purpose in the mystery of his divine plan. "'For my thoughts are not your thoughts, neither are your ways my ways,' declares the Lord" (Isa. 55:8). Try as we might, we will never see life with God's eyes from our position on earth. Our human perspective, which is bound by time and space, tells us that suffering is loathsome and that death is loss. From God's eternal viewpoint, however, suffering is a gift granted to make us more like our Creator (Phil. 1:29; 3:10), and death is a gain. "Precious in the sight of the Lord is the death of his saints," reads Psalm 116:15.

Although this knowledge may offer little consolation when we are in the midst of trials, we need to remember that God calls us, his children, to do no more than his own Son, who suffered our deepest anguishes. "As sure as ever God puts his children in the furnace,"

68

said Charles Spurgeon, "he will be in the furnace with them."[6]

Christ's suffering and death on the cross were the culmination of his life, the perfection of his mission of salvation. Because we are made in the image of God, we can expect no less in our own lives. Dorothy Sayers examined this duality of suffering in *Creed or Chaos?*:

> For whatever reason God chose to make man as he is—limited and suffering and subject to sorrows and death—he had the honesty and the courage to take his own medicine. Whatever game he is playing with his creation, he has kept his own rules and played fair. He can exact nothing from us that he has not exacted from himself. He has himself gone through the whole of human experience, from the trivial irritations of family life and the cramping restrictions of hard work and lack of money to the worst horrors of pain, humiliation, defeat, despair and death. When he was a man, he played the man. He was born in poverty and died in disgrace and thought it was well worth while.[7]

Redemptive Suffering

We must accept that God, in his sovereignty, planned for life to embrace both pleasure and pain, both good and evil, both wheat and weeds. "Let both grow together until the harvest," Jesus taught in Matthew 13:30. He explained that even though the weeds had been sown by an enemy, to uproot them would harm the wheat growing alongside. Indeed, the "weeds" are *necessary* to compel us to become closer to God, to develop in holiness. We fail to grow without pain and suffering as our prods.

Because good and evil exist side by side, the good is often tragically affected by the bad. We can take comfort, however, in the knowledge that nothing happens outside of God's sovereignty and that God can bring good out of all things, if we allow it. God not only grieves with us in our sorrows, but he also is always at work to redeem the suffering of his children (Rom. 8:28–29).

This concept of redemptive suffering is poignantly portrayed in an analogy of refined metal by Arthur T. Pierson:

> Our Father, who seeks to perfect His saints in holiness, knows the value of the refiner's fire. It is with the most precious metals that the assayer takes the most pains, and subjects them to the hot fire, because such fires melt the metal, and only the molten mass releases its alloy or takes perfectly its new form in the mould. The old refiner never leaves his crucible, but sits down by it, lest there should be one excessive degree of heat to mar the metal. But as soon as he skims from the surface the last of the dross, and sees his own face reflected, he puts out the fire.[8]

Not Why But What

Sometimes when we question the why of suffering, we struggle with verses from the Bible that seem to promise divine protection, such as "No harm befalls the righteous" (Prov. 12:21) and "If you make the Most High your dwelling ... then no harm will befall you" (Ps. 91:9–10). Indeed, some today have seized these words and have preached that "good" Christians are

70

immune to troubles and that sin is the cause of all problems. Every sniffle or cough, then, is a sign of wrongdoing, and a calamity signifies a terrible transgression.

These promises, however, were written to the Israelites, who thought very differently than we do today in our highly individualistic culture. While we think of ourselves as single units, the Israelites saw themselves collectively and understood these words to apply to their nation. When we try to claim them as individual promises, we end up with a "health and wealth," "name it and claim it," "grab it and stab it" religion that is self-serving instead of God-honoring. We give our obedience to get God's blessings. This kind of thinking also causes speculation about the spiritual lives of those who suffer affliction.

Jesus himself pointed out the error of this thinking when his disciples brought up the question of sin in regard to a blind man. "Who sinned, this man or his parents, that he was born blind?" they asked (John 9:2). Jesus responded that sin was not responsible for the tragedy. "But this happened so that the work of God might be displayed in his life," was his reply, which he followed with an admonition to do God's work on earth (John 9:3–4).

The Rev. Harvey Kiekover has speculated that the entire thrust of Jesus' answer is our role in the suffering of others. He suggested that the period used by modern translators after "life" is misplaced. "The original manuscripts of the gospel contained no punctuation. . . . A simple change in the punctuation of Jesus' answer makes a rather profound difference in the meaning of his words," he wrote. "Try reading Jesus' words this way: 'But, in order that the work of God might be displayed in his life, it is necessary for us to work the works of the one sending me, while it is day.' The man is blind, Jesus says; now what are you going to do about it?"[9]

Perhaps the most important question we can ask about suffering is not *why* but *what*. What are we going to do about suffering? Instead of simply analyzing its origin, we need to deal with its presence. People are born blind; they are born with AIDS; they are injured by life; they suffer the effects of evil. God calls us to comfort, to encourage, to instruct, to serve, and to minister to those who are hurting. Are we going to sit in judgment (of God or other people), or are we going to do the works of him who sent Jesus and who now sends us?

SIX

A Purple Rage—
Bitterness and
Depression

When we fail to deal effectively with our anger and sadness, these emotions can combine to create an internal, malevolent blend of feelings. Instead of remaining reactions to specific situations, anger (red) and sadness (blue) join forces to bring about an emotional state that is difficult to change.

When more anger than sadness is present and the anger is directed at others, this emotional state is known as bitterness. When more sadness than anger is present and the anger is directed at ourselves, the result is psychological depression (as opposed to endogenous depression, which has its roots in the biochemistry of the brain). Bitterness and depression, with their roots in unresolved anger and sadness, make for a *bad* blend of emotions and internal rage.

HOW BITTERNESS AND DEPRESSION DEVELOP

Ruby and her brother, Albert, trace their lingering anger and sadness to their childhood. They grew up in a single-parent home where they could do nothing to please their mother. Ruby was often confined to her bedroom for failing to dust the furniture or wash the dishes well enough. Albert was beaten every time he overslept or was late from school.

The worst abuse occurred at Christmas, however, when Mother placed brightly wrapped packages for her children under the tree, only to threaten to return them to the store if the children misbehaved. Each year she found a reason to take away every present. As a result, Ruby and Albert never received a Christmas present from their mother. Their natural reactions were sadness due to the loss of a normal childhood and anger at their mother for depriving them of it.

When they reached their thirties, the siblings experienced even greater distress than when they were children. Albert had never been able to forgive his mother for her injustices against him, and the bitterness he felt toward her spilled into every thought. The bitterness overflowed into his spiritual life because Albert also blamed God for allowing his mother to treat him so badly. Ruby, on the other hand, blamed herself instead of her mother or God, thinking she somehow must have deserved her rotten upbringing. Ruby contemplated suicide to escape her depression.

Even though Ruby and Albert both experienced unresolved anger and sadness, these emotions were revealed differently in their lives. Albert was bitter because he blamed others for his problems, which fueled his anger; Ruby was depressed because she blamed herself, which contributed to her sadness. Blame is a major component of bitterness and depression, whether it is directed at ourselves, others, or God. It keeps us from working through anger and sadness.

Blaming Others

Accepting that things often go badly, without pointing a finger of blame, has become unpopular in our culture. No matter what our problem, we can find someone else to hold responsible, whether it be a compulsive mother, an alcoholic father, a drunk driver, a drug pusher, or an unimaginative teacher.

The real problem with blaming others is that it prevents us from getting over our anger. As long as we blame others, we give them control over our lives. This creates more anger. We may not even realize we are blaming others for disappointments in our lives. But if we feel bitter toward others, we need to examine why we continue to hold them responsible for our lives.

Blaming God

It can be so easy to blame God. After all, he *is* in control of the universe. And he's been taking blame for a long time. When God asked Adam about his sin, Adam replied, "The woman *you put here with me*—she gave me some fruit from the tree, and I ate it" (Gen. 3:12, emphasis added). Adam suggested that the sin was God's fault because God placed Eve on earth.

We, too, often hold God responsible for our ills. To keep the right perspective, we need to remember that what God intends for good is often thwarted by our own mistakes and a fallen earth. At some point we need to take responsibility for our own choices and accept the reality of living in a broken world where people often wound one another profoundly.

Blaming Ourselves

Even when we take responsibility for our bad decisions, we need to stop short of blaming ourselves. If you keep kicking yourself for your past mistakes, your feet will be too busy to take you forward with your life. We need to remember the apostle Paul's instructions to the church at Philippi that we should be "forgetting what is behind and straining toward what is ahead" (Phil. 3:13). In other words, we need to forgive ourselves.

Sometimes we take responsibility for choices that we were never allowed to make. When we blame ourselves for the behavior of others, we assume an unrealistic and self-destructive sense of control. For example, Ruby saw herself as somehow responsible for the abuse and neglect she experienced, as if there were something wrong with her that made her deserve mistreatment.

People who are abused often come to expect the abuse, blaming themselves for the pathology of the abuser. They must learn to see themselves as children of God who are worthy of respect. Only as we come to see ourselves as worthy of regard will we be unwilling to accept blame for the actions of others.

The Shame of Blame

No matter whom we blame—others, God, or ourselves—the effect is the same. Blame keeps us holding on to our hurts and invites bitterness and depression to take up residence in our hearts. Once these guests move in, they won't leave easily. Indeed, many people remain bitter and depressed because they are unwilling to work at change.

BANISHING BITTERNESS

Christians often struggle with bitterness because they are loathe to admit they have angry, let alone bitter, feelings. Before bitter feelings can be defeated, therefore, they must be recognized. Keep a diary of your upset or angry thoughts for a week and see what patterns emerge. What do you find yourself ruminating about? What people continue to be associated with painful memories? This grudge list will help you identify those who have wronged you whom you have not forgiven. Talking over hurtful situations with a trustworthy friend also will help you verbalize your feelings and discover where bitterness remains.

Although facing bitterness is painful, it is not as distressing as allowing bitterness to remain. We need to recognize just how destructive this festering feeling is. In *None of These Diseases,* Dr. S. I. McMillen vividly described what "thoughts that fume like nitric acid and corrode as deeply" can do to us: "The moment I start hating a man, I become his slave. I can't enjoy my work any more because he even controls my thoughts. . . . I can't escape his tyrannical grasp on my mind."[1]

Perhaps when we realize the high cost that bitterness extracts from us, we might be more willing to pay the price of forgiveness. When we forgive, we must exonerate others of fault, no matter how terribly they acted. Only this act of forgiveness, however, will free us to give up our bitterness and take back control of our lives. Like Jesus, we need to say, "Forgive . . . for they do not know what they are doing" (Luke 23:34).

A friend once told us that she had been counseled by her pastor not to forgive her father, who had sexually abused her when she was a child. Because the father had sought forgiveness from neither his daughter nor God, the pastor reasoned that our friend was not required to forgive him and that for her to forgive in this situation would be to do "more than God could do." We believe this advice fails to take into account the healing that forgiveness brings to the forgiver. We must forgive to release our anger.

This concept is illustrated in the way that Dwight David Eisenhower handled forgiveness. "When Ike was angry at someone, he would write the person's name on a piece of paper and throw it in the trash. This sort of spiritual calisthenics takes a lot of work, but the point of forgiveness is to let *yourself* off the hook, let down *your* burden," wrote Benjamin J. Stein.[2]

Lewis Smedes called forgiveness "God's invention for coming to terms with a world in which, despite their best intentions, people are unfair to each other and hurt each other deeply. [God] began by forgiving us. And he invites us all to forgive each other."[3]

Forgiveness becomes easier when we realize that the act of forgiving does not excuse someone's behavior or lessen the impact of the evil. Instead it is being willing to bear the price of the iniquity ourselves, just as Jesus did on the cross when he forgave us. As David Augsburger has noted, "The man who forgives pays a tremendous price—the price of the evil he forgives. If the state pardons a criminal, society bears the burden of the criminal's deed. If I break a priceless heirloom that you treasure and you forgive me, you bear the loss and I go free. In forgiveness, you bear your own anger and wrath at the sin of another."[4]

Forgiving also requires us to relinquish our vengeful feelings. This can be difficult, particularly when we have been unjustly hurt. At those times, holding on to our anger can feel so right. We may even come to cherish our feelings of bitterness toward another. We need to remember, however, that meting out justice is God's responsibility. In fact, the Bible tells us that when we take revenge, we leave no room for God's wrath (Rom. 12:19). Instead we are commanded to love our enemies, with the hope that our love will turn them from their wrongdoing.

Forgiving must also be followed by forgetting. Unfortunately, the two are not wrapped together as a package deal. When we forgive, we don't develop amnesia. The wrongs we forgive will continue to come to mind, and we must actively choose to forego ruminating about them.

This type of forgetting is not simply denial, however, because it involves recognizing our pain in a new light. It requires us to choose to see our hurt in terms of a broken world, where we all—even our offenders—act out of our pain. If we choose not to forget, then we really have not forgiven, suggested Henry Ward Beecher. " 'I can forgive, but I cannot forget,' is another way of saying, 'I cannot forgive.' "5

DEFEATING DEPRESSION

Like bitterness, psychological depression (as opposed to endogenous depression) also has anger and sadness at its core. But this time the proportions are reversed, with anger taking a back seat to sadness.

Many depressed people are surprised that anger plays any role at all in their depression. Yet most psychologists would agree that virtually all depression has repressed anger at its base, anger that is turned inward. Psychiatrist Paul Meier believes that poorly handled anger is the cause of about ninety-five percent of psychological depressions.[6] Fear, frustration, loss, and guilt may also contribute to depressed feelings.

Once viewed as a disorder of middle and old age, depression now shows significant increases among adolescents and young adults. Women are two to three times more likely to suffer from depression, possibly because women in general are less effective in dealing with their anger.[7]

Although we all have depressed feelings from time to time, clinical depression refers to episodes of depressed moods lasting at least two weeks. Its symptoms commonly include change in appetite, sleep disturbance, pacing, hand-wringing, slowed movements, monotone speech, and difficulty thinking or concentrating. Depressed people often experience decreased energy because their repressed anger is associated with repressing and blunting their other feelings as well. Feelings of worthlessness and guilt are also common, as those who are depressed internalize their anger and blame themselves.

Sometimes people who are depressed become further distressed because they are ashamed of their feelings. Somewhere the notion got started that spiritual Christians are immune to depression. The idea did not spring from the Bible, however, because many of its heroes struggled with depression, including Moses, Jonah, Jeremiah, David, and Elijah. Indeed, it is through Elijah's depression that we are able to learn how God himself treated depression. Not surprisingly, it is the approach that counselors emulate today.

A Purple Rage—Bitterness and Depression

In 1 Kings 18 we read about the prophet Elijah's tremendous triumph over the prophets of Baal at Mount Carmel. In the next chapter, we discover Elijah lying under a tree praying for God to take his life. The same steps that God used to help Elijah rediscover the joy of life can be used to help ourselves or others who are struggling with depression.

1. God provided for Elijah's physical needs.

Elijah was physically drained after his encounter with the prophets of Baal. Not only had he faced 450 leaders of an opposing religion, but he had also just run twenty-five miles into Jezreel after his victory. What Elijah most needed was food, drink, and time to sleep, which is just what God provided for him via an angel.

Dr. John Stott has noted that the Christian's chief occupational hazards are depression and discouragement.[8] Like Elijah, we can become "weary of well-doing" and in need of some quiet time under the juniper tree. We especially need to guard against doing too much *for* God and failing to spend enough time *with* God. When our spiritual activities displace our quiet time and prayer, we fail to allow God the opportunity to recharge our spiritual batteries. This opens us to depression.

Another physical need when we are depressed may be medication. When depression is associated with biochemical changes in the brain, medication may be required to correct the resulting imbalance in the brain's neurotransmitters. Depression may even be caused by a reaction to medications given for other physical problems, such as high blood pressure. Therefore, if you are experiencing severe and prolonged

81

depression, and especially if you cannot trace it back to the original sad and angry feelings, you should seek a professional evaluation.

2. God recognized Elijah's depression and asked Elijah to recognize it also.

God asked Elijah, "What are you doing here?" That is not a question that depressed people want to answer. They usually don't know what has brought them to the point of depression, and often they are too dejected to care. But facing up to depressed feelings is the first step toward changing them. We must be willing to muster the strength to recognize and confront unresolved feelings. We need to think about what has made us frustrated, hurt, sad, afraid, or angry and then consider what desire or goal in our lives is being blocked. We must recognize our feelings before we can begin to change them. They will not disappear quietly into the night.

3. God straightened out Elijah's thinking.

Elijah told God that he was the only one still faithful in Israel. God gently reminded him that the number of those who had not bowed to Baal actually was closer to seven thousand. Elijah's tendency to see life from a negative perspective is common in those who are depressed. Depressed people tend to see a half-empty glass of water instead of a half-full glass. They see mountains instead of molehills, boulders instead of stepping stones, and walls instead of doorways. Depressed feelings affect our ability to process information clearly, resulting in a distortion of reality. If we are depressed, we need someone to challenge and correct our thinking.

4. *God got Elijah busy again.*

Depressed people often believe that life is hopeless and unfair and that they are worthless. It is as if they see through a dark, gloomy filter that removes the color and joy from life.

While these negative thoughts pass through most of our minds at one time or another, we are generally able to shake them off and think about other things. Studies have shown that depressed people, however, are unable to distract themselves from these thoughts. They "tend to be withdrawn and to stay in a bleak setting devoid of any positive distractions," observed psychologist Richard Wenzlaff.[9]

His research suggests that when the ability to control negative thoughts breaks down, depression results. Perhaps this is one reason the Bible admonishes Christians to think about positive things instead: "whatever is true ... noble ... right ... pure ... lovely ... admirable ... praiseworthy—think about such things" (Phil. 4:8).

Wenzlaff proposed that depressed people need to do things to distract themselves from unhappy thoughts. "Depressed people could benefit from getting into situations they enjoy: going to sporting events, or seeing an uplifting movie or reading something funny," he suggested. The worst reaction to depression is to isolate ourselves from things that can bring us fulfillment and joy.

God did not let Elijah stay in a cave in Horeb. Instead he gave him a few small tasks—nothing too taxing, but things that would distract Elijah from self-pity and depression and get him back on his feet. Likewise, we need someone to push us out of our cocoons when we wrap ourselves with depressed thoughts.

5. God gave Elijah a friend and confidant.

Christians often try to hide their depression from others, thinking it is a sign of spiritual failure. They put on their "I'm fine; how are you?" mask, which only adds to their feelings of depression. While we don't have to advertise our feelings, we must make sure that we share them with at least one close friend. Having someone who will listen to us may mean the difference between transitory depressed feelings and clinical depression.

For Elijah, that friend was Elisha, who one day finished Elijah's ministry. If you know people who are depressed, make a point of spending time with them. It is so easy to neglect them because they are not much fun to be with and they may say they would rather be alone, anyway. But even if your visits are difficult, don't give up on someone who is depressed.

SEVEN

A Streak of Yellow— Fear

The story is told that one night long ago a desert traveler met Fear and Plague, who were on their way to Baghdad to kill ten thousand persons. The traveler asked if Plague would be responsible for the deaths. "I can't take credit for more than a few hundred," replied Plague. "My friend, Fear, will take care of the others."

Today, Fear continues his tour of terror. Because Plague's journeys have been limited, however, Fear travels extensively with other companions, such as Crime, Financial Insecurity, War, Cancer, Abuse, Divorce, and Failure. Sometimes Fear can be easily identified because he uses a specific name, such as acrophobia (fear of heights) or cynophobia (fear of dogs), both of which rank among our top ten fears.[1]

Other times, Fear attacks without a proper introduction. A nameless terror creates a general feeling of anxiety that can be just as damaging as a phobia with a fancy name. In fact, this state of fear is often more difficult to treat because its roots must be identified before the fear can be confronted.

Not only do we live in a world fraught with risk and

danger, but we also have a media network prone to report calamity in graphic, and sometimes sensational, detail. When we exhaust our personal list of worries, we only need to open the newspaper or turn on the television or radio to encounter a myriad more. Our son watched the evening news with us for the first time when he was in kindergarten. His response was, "Can we pray more?"

Fear was one of the earliest negative emotions experienced by Adam in the Garden of Eden. His first recorded words in the Bible were, "I was afraid" (Gen. 3:10). Unfortunately, fear is also considered to be the most limiting emotion. It can cause tunnel vision, in which we block out everything from view except our fear. As a result, our thinking becomes rigid and concentrated. Fear is also linked with insomnia, depression, inactivity, forgetfulness, and dread. It results in more than seventy million anti-anxiety prescriptions written by physicians yearly. We don't like to feel afraid.

FEAR TO THE RESCUE

We couldn't survive without fear, however. God intended this emotion as a means of protection; it prepares our bodies for action when we are in immediate danger.

Pretend for a moment that one dark evening you are strolling down the avenue when you are startled by a shady individual wearing a hockey mask shrieking toward you. Being vaguely familiar with a series of grotesque films about such a character, you immediately feel afraid. Your brain sends the fear alarm to your body, which prepares you for flight or fight: your heart beats faster, your blood pressure rises, your muscles tense, your digestive functions slow, you breathe faster, your hair follicles tighten, and epinephrine pours into your bloodstream, enabling you to outdistance your assailant.

In this case fear may have saved your life. Henry Ward Beecher called this fear "a kind of bell or gong which rings the mind into quick life and avoidance on the approach of danger."[2]

FEAR AS THE ATTACKER

The negative side of fear exerts its power when our immediate fears become our future fears. If this episode on the avenue were to keep you from leaving your home for fear of a repeat occurrence, then fear is doing its dirty work on you. You become afraid that this, or something worse, may happen to you in the future.

Women who have been raped experience this future fear often, as expressed by these quotes from an article on rape in *Woman's Day*: "I'm afraid to come home alone. . . . I can't go outside after dark, not even to take out the garbage. . . . I still think about what happened at least once daily. . . . I'm still not the person I was—I've lost my zest for life."[3] For these women, fear of the future controls their lives.

FEAR AS THE DECEIVER

Fear can also control our lives even if we are *never* in danger. Suppose that in the avenue incident you ran for your life, only to realize a few moments later that the date was October 31—Halloween! The threat was not to your state of being but to the stash of Milky Ways in your purse. Even though you weren't in danger, however, your body responded as if you were. You still experienced the rush of adrenalin and the pumping heart.

The point of this example is that we believe what we tell ourselves. If we believe we are threatened in some way, our body will prime itself for action. These threats may be to our physical health or, more often, to our emotional well-being. If we are afraid that our spouse may be engaged in an affair or that our money won't last the month or that our friends don't really like us, we will experience the physical responses needed for flight or fight, even if our beliefs are inaccurate.

FEAR AS THE DESTROYER

The problem with threats to our emotional well-being (whether real or imagined) is that they don't respond well to flight or fight. Increased blood pressure does not make us more attractive to our mate or friends, nor does adrenalin increase our checkbook balance. Instead we have all this energy building inside us as a response to fear, and it has nowhere to go. Trapped inside our bodies, this boost of adrenalin prevents our bodies from relaxing. As our muscles tighten, pain is produced. In fact, the literal meaning of the word worry is "to strangle or give pain." When Franklin Delano Roosevelt noted, "We have nothing to fear but fear itself," shortly after becoming president in 1933, he was more accurate than he knew.[4] Even a little fear can be a terrible thing.

FEAR NOT

So what is the solution to our fears? God gives us his answer in just one word: don't. The Bible records

God telling us to "fear not" more than eighty times. But we can't obey this directive just by saying, "Okay, I will not be afraid." Fear won't retreat into the corner. In order to change the color of fear in our life, we have to change the thinking and behavior underneath its yellow exterior.

A New Look at Fear

Truth often has little to do with the way we think or what we believe. Rather, much of our thinking is based on untruths—inaccuracies we believe about ourselves, others, and God. Unfortunately, untruths create a great deal of fear in our lives.

Sharon, a bright thirty-three-year-old, wakes several times during the night to check on her young son. Sharon says she is afraid he may stop breathing or become ill. Her perception is not based on any truth about her son; he has never suffered from more than an ear infection. Sharon's need to check on her son actually stems from her fear that she is an inadequate mother, a belief passed on to Sharon from her mother. For Sharon to change her thinking, she must learn to base her thoughts on the truth: that she really is a good mother, that her son is not in danger at night, and that she can trust her son to God.

Basing our thoughts on the truth is a difficult process for us because we live in an imperfect world where we are often treated badly and unfairly. All of us grew up believing untruths about ourselves, others, and God. We may have learned that we are unworthy of God's love, that others are to be feared, or that God is not good.

Distorted thinking has several common motifs,

which David Burns discussed in his book, *Feeling Good, The New Mood Therapy*.[5] One is overgeneralization, which means we take one negative event and see it as a never-ending pattern of failure. Another is the mental filter, in which we dwell on one negative detail to the point that it darkens our perception of life. A third common motif is all-or-nothing thinking, in which we see things either as black or white, good or bad.

Fortunately, we can take steps to minimize the distortion in our views of ourselves, our world, and our God. We can learn to sharpen, redirect, and expand our vision.

Sharpening Our Vision. We can sharpen our vision by focusing our perceptions on the truth. We need to measure our fear against the odds of it happening. How likely is it that you might lose your job? What is the chance that you have a serious illness? Pastor Donald Shelby pointed out that while some of our fears are legitimate, "most of them are imagined and needless. Know the difference. Know what to fear."[6]

Instead of wringing our hands and speculating on the future, we can take the future into our hands. How? By investigating the basis of our fear and listing the hard facts relevant to it. If our fear seems to be based in reality, we need to think through what we can do to prevent it from happening. The best antidote for fear is a sense of control. For example, if your fact-finding mission turns up a high probability that you may be laid off from your job, don't fret your way to unemployment. Check out severance packages, mail out résumés, and spread the word that you are in the market for a new job.

When we are unsure whether a fear is based on truth, we can ask a friend. Friends can be great reality checkers for us. For example, if Sharon would ask someone other than her mother to rate her parenting skills, she would probably hear that she is doing a good job. When we are too close to a problem to see it in proper perspective, friends can provide a more objective point of view. They can help remove some of the smudges blurring our vision. If you don't have a friend you can trust, or if your sense of reality needs a major overhaul, then you may want to seek the help of a trained counselor.

Sometimes we unwittingly hang onto our fears because we receive some sort of payback for them. Even though fear itself is distressing, it sometimes can carry a reward with it. For example, Evonne suffered from agoraphobia (fear of being away from home), which curiously began to develop at the same time as her marital problems. At some subconscious level, Evonne knew that as long as she was unable to leave home, her husband would not leave her.

In dealing with fear, we have to take a sharp look at ourselves. Are we receiving some sort of compensation that keeps us tied to our fear? It could be the attention of a loved one, release from responsibilities, or the avoidance of a pain greater than fear.

Redirecting Our Vision. The more we think about our worries and fears, the more anxious we become. Conversely, allowing our thoughts to be redirected is directly linked to a decrease in anxiety.

Exercise is a wonderful diversion for anxiety. A vigorous aerobic workout corresponds with a drop in anxiety, although "it may not be the exercise per se, but the distraction from the cares and worries of the day," said researcher William P. Morgan.[7] While we have not yet identified the physiological mechanism by which the body transmutes exercise into anxiety reduction, studies show that regular exercisers may be able to reduce not just state anxiety (how you feel right now), but also trait anxiety (how you feel most of the time).

Whether we walk aerobically or simply take a walk with a good friend, we can use the time to direct our thoughts from our fears. Curling up with an exciting book may prove to provide the same amount of anxiety-reduction as curling weights. The point is this: pursue an activity that will take your mind off your worries.

Meditation is also valuable for redirecting thoughts. Instead of focusing upon our problems and fears, we direct our mind to concentrate on something else. The Bible provides numerous examples of God's people *filling* their minds with thoughts of God and his power and goodness. This type of meditation differs from that found in other religions, where the goal is to *empty* the mind. The Bible talks of meditations on God's unfailing love, his promises, his mighty deeds, his wonders, his wonderful works, and his precepts. If you experience difficulty concentrating, try meditating for short periods of time, especially before you fall asleep. Its rewards are well worth the struggle.

Humor is another helpful diversion for dealing with anxiety. "If you can laugh at yourself, you won't take your problems too seriously," advised Dr. Nick Stinnett, a professor of human development and family studies at the University of Alabama.[8] He and his associates found that good-natured humor promotes a positive outlook, alleviates anxiety, and reduces tension. Take time to read a funny book, see a funny movie, or simply share laughter with friends and family.

Expanding Our Vision. Since fears have a nasty way of keeping us focused upon ourselves, they tend to give us a bad case of tunnel vision. When we concentrate on a problem, we allow it to infect every part of our lives. To get out of the tunnel, we need to practice seeing our fears from an expanded and more reliable perspective. We suggest the best perspective for the Christian is found in God. In order to see our life from his point of view, we have to expand our vision in three directions: back, up, and ahead.

Look Back. Your past is an important part of who you are today. If you were called stupid as a child, you may be afraid your ideas are still unworthy of expression. If you were rejected by a loved one once, you may fear it will happen again. If at one time you experienced trauma, you may lie awake reliving the event again and again. These past experiences color the way you think about yourself and your world. Until they are laid to rest, the pain and hurts that you once experienced can continue to haunt your present life.

You cannot erase your bad experiences, but you can change the way you think about them. Share your concerns with a trustworthy person who can offer you insights into your experiences. As you spend time with others and with God, you can learn to see your past through a new perspective.

Sometimes we have buried the cause of our anxiety so deeply that identifying the roots of our anxious feelings is very difficult. For example, in another case involving agoraphobia, Gretchen thought she had no idea why she was afraid to be in public places. After weeks of intensive therapy, she discovered that her phobia had generalized from a fear of bridges. A few years earlier she had driven her acutely ill son to a hospital, not knowing if he would survive the trip. Her route traversed a three-mile-long, one-hundred-foot-high bridge. The extreme anxiety she felt that day stayed with her, increasing its grip on her life until she was unable to leave her home. Once Gretchen figured out the genesis of her phobia, she was able to work on resolving it.

If you cannot identify the source of your anxiety on your own or with the help of friends, counseling may be necessary to enable you to unearth, and then confront, your fear.

Look Up. "In general, the optimist is less afraid," wrote Martin E. P. Seligman, Ph.D., author of *Learned Optimism*.[9] Christians especially have a firm foundation for optimism. When we look up, we find our eyes on Jesus. As we look up to Jesus' love and to his purpose, we take our eyes off our own fears and circumstances. When the apostle Peter tried to walk on the water to reach Jesus, he did not begin to sink until he took his eyes off Jesus and focused on the storm. Peter became afraid because he saw the power of the storm instead of the power of his Lord. Jesus' comforting words in that passage can help us today with our fears: "Take courage! It is I" (Matt. 14:27).

No matter what our circumstances, we can put them into perspective by looking past them and up into the eyes and arms of God. One of our favorite lines in the Bible that addresses God's ability to take care of his children is found in Numbers 11:23. There God asks simply, "Is the Lord's arm too short?" We need to remember that God's arm stretches all the way from heaven to earth, that it doesn't dangle helplessly from a cloud. Whenever we fail to look up to God, however, we limit his power to a "short arm." The next time fear takes control over you, put it in perspective by picturing the ludicrous image of a short, dangling arm in the sky. If you believe that God is all-powerful, then believe that his power is enough to help you.

In our own experience, we find encouragement as we read and meditate upon God's Word. We need to be frequently reminded that God (and God alone) is our protector, our refuge, and our defender. As we know and experience how perfectly God loves us, we empower his perfect love to help us with our fear.

Look Ahead. Søren Kierkegaard called anxiety "the next day."[10] Indeed, the fear of tomorrow is responsible for ruining many todays. We cringe at the thought of the dangers and disasters lurking around our future. Many times we may wonder how we could survive if we lost our health, our spouse, our children, or our financial security. "The best thing about the future," said Abraham Lincoln, "is that it comes only one day at a time."[11] When we take on too many tomorrows at once, fear robs us of our future before it is even ours.

No amount of money or planning can give us security that tomorrow will be good. Howard Hughes was one of the richest men in the world, yet he died a captive of fear. He was so terrified of germs that he spent his last years inside a sterile room.[12] No matter how hard we try, we cannot peer into our future. That is why the Bible warns us against worrying about tomorrow. "Who of you by worrying can add a single hour to his life?" Jesus asked in Luke 12:25.

Luke used an interesting word in this passage to describe worrying, one that is not used elsewhere in the New Testament. The Greek for it is *meteōros*, which literally means "high in the air." Perhaps Luke was

95

warning against letting our minds go high in the air searching for security, zooming around like a meteor.

When our son, Matthew, was three years old, he could not bear to be without his mother. If she even walked into another room when he was playing, he would race throughout the house searching for her, shrieking all the while. In his frenzy he usually ran right past her. He did not understand that she would never leave him alone, that even when she was out of his sight, she was still nearby.

How often we Christians do the same thing. When we don't "feel" God because our situation seems so desolate, we become terrified and go on a desperate hunt for our security, fretting all the while. Our minds end up "high in the air," where they are easily swept away by strong wind currents, taking us farther from God and adding to our fears. In our panic, we usually race right past him, forgetting that he has promised never to leave us.

The next time you feel your head floating off, full of anxiety and worry, pull it back down. Despite uncertainty, we can still look forward to tomorrow because of two promises we find in the Bible.

The first promise is that God is in control. George Müeller was so confident of God's control that when his wife died, he said he would not bring her back even if it were the easiest thing in the world to do. "God Himself has done it," he said. "We are satisfied with Him."[13] As you believe that God loves you and that he has the power to work everything for your good, you will be better able to arrest your fear of the future. Remember, the best antidote for fear is a sense of control. Even when you seem to have little control over your life, you can know that God does.

Unfortunately, our society has lost much of its reverence for God and his power. Because we no longer fear God (in the sense of revering him), we fear everything else. Today God is often depicted as powerless or fickle or easily manipulated. Compare this view with how the Israelites saw God. When Moses prepared to approach God on Mount Sinai, the people said, "Speak to us yourself and we will listen. But do not have God speak to us or we will die" (Ex. 20:19). Moses replied with a seeming paradox: "Do not be afraid . . . so that the fear of God will be with you." In other words, we never have to fear the love of our heavenly Father, yet we need to remember who he is. Our respect and reverence for God are what free us from other fears.

Another promise God gives us concerning our future is that of his grace. There is nothing that can prepare us for tragedy except faith in God's supernatural grace to help us in our time of need.

Horatio Spafford experienced almost inconceivable calamity in his lifetime. The attorney and his family lost all their possessions in the great Chicago fire of 1871. Just two years after that disaster, a French steamer carrying Spafford's wife and four of his five children suffered a mid-ocean collision. Ten days after the accident he received this cable from his wife: "Saved alone." The *Ville de Havre* had sunk to the bottom of the sea in thirty minutes, and nearly all on board had been lost. Spafford's wife had been found floating in the water by one of the sailors.

Yet out of that tragedy came one of our most loved hymns, "It Is Well with My Soul," which Spafford penned in commemoration of the death of his children. Only God's grace can account for Spafford's ability to write these lines: "When peace, like a river, attendeth

97

my way, When sorrows like sea billows roll; Whatever my lot, Thou hast taught me to say, It is well, it is well with my soul."[14]

CONFRONTING FEAR

While changing the way we think about our fears is important, at some point we also have to make changes in our behavior. We have to actively face our fears if we are ever to leave them behind. One of the best ways to feed a fear is to avoid what you fear. Unfortunately, dodging fears is also the most popular response. We are afraid to speak in public, so we never do it. We have a fear of flying, so we take the train. We fear the truth about a relationship, so we never ask. This kind of avoidance only serves to increase our fears, because our imagination endows our fear with more power over us.

Sometimes the best approach to overcoming a fear is to confront it directly. Recently we visited friends who had just moved to a farm. Their three-year-old son was riding a horse led by his father when the mare stepped on a puppy and reared, throwing the child to the ground. While neither the dog nor the child was seriously hurt, the puppy ran away and stayed away from the horse. The boy, however, wiped his tears, brushed off his pants, and asked to be put back on the horse. The little guy thwarted a fear of horses by hopping right back in the saddle.

Confronting fears does not have to be done in one gulp. If you have a serious fear of snakes, don't bring one home for a pet. Taking little steps toward your object of fear, called desensitization, is easier and just as effective. You might try a few weeks of reading about snakes, then looking at their pictures, then visiting them at the zoo, then touching one.

Prayer is another activity we can use to confront our fears. With prayer, we harness our weakness to God's yoke of strength. Prayer can help us work through our worries before they mount up with wings of terror against us. Prayer is "a powerful and effectual worry-remover," wrote William Sadler.[15]

Prayer is the activity that Paul suggested to the Philippians to combat anxiety. He wrote, "Do not be anxious about anything, but in everything, by prayer and petition, with thanksgiving, present your requests to God" (Phil. 4:6). The key words here are "with thanksgiving." When we pray, we can thank God ahead of time—thank him for being in control, for loving us perfectly, for providing for our needs, and for giving us grace that is sufficient for any circumstances.

We can turn any worry into a prayer. When we realize that we are fretting about something, we can choose to change the direction of our thought. Instead of thinking, "I'm afraid the test results on my medical exam will reveal cancer," we can change the worry into a prayer: "Lord, thank you that you already know the test results. No matter what my future, I can trust that your love and grace will always be with me. I never have to be afraid when you are in control."

Worries drain vitality from us; prayers tap God's vitality. Worries are negative; prayers are positive. Worries are useless; prayers are productive. Can we give any reason to waste our life with something that is draining, negative, and useless? Worry, someone once said, is like a rocking chair. It gives you something to do, but it doesn't get you anywhere. Another writer described it this way: "Worry doesn't empty the day of its trouble, but only of its strength."[16]

"He only is rich who owns the day," wrote Ralph Waldo Emerson. "Write it on your heart that every day is the best day in the year."[17] The Lord has given you today, and his Spirit gives you the power to own it. Don't allow worry and anxiety to steal your precious hours. Fear can rob you of your joy in life only with your permission.

EIGHT

How Turning Green Brings Double Trouble—Envy

When our son was three years old, he and his six-year-old sister enjoyed pretending to be spies from outer space. One morning we noticed them lurking behind a closet door. As they spotted us, we heard Matthew warn Joelle, "Oh, no! Double trouble—human beings!"

While double trouble may or may not accurately describe our species, it certainly is an apt depiction of one of our emotions—envy (James 3:16).

Not only does envy bring double trouble, but it also stems from double emotions—desire and anger. While neither feeling is necessarily destructive by itself, when the two are doubled up they create a particularly toxic condition. When we desire what others have—and become hostile toward them because of it—we open wide Pandora's box of problems. "Envy can ruin reputations, split churches, and cause murders. Envy can shrink our circle of friends, ruin our business, and dwarf our souls," wrote Billy Graham.[1]

Envy is not a basic emotion. It is a nurtured, sinful emotion. It well deserves its inclusion in the seven

deadly sins. The Bible is brimming with the consequences of envy. Cain murdered Abel because of it; it
led Aaron and Miriam to oppose Moses; Saul lived a
tortured life due to his envy of David; King Ahab
murdered Naboth the Jezreelite due to envy over his
garden; and Jesus was handed over to Pilate because of
it. Envy was also the downfall of Satan, who was cast
from heaven for envying God himself, for trying to
become "like the Most High" (Isa. 14:14).

ENVY'S COMPANIONS

Perhaps because envy can have such deadly results
for ourselves as well as others, we are warned repeatedly in the Bible to rid ourselves of it. We must be
careful here, however, to draw a distinction between
envy and jealousy. While these words are often used
interchangeably in our culture, they are actually two
distinct emotions.

Jealousy involves a rival for affection and the threat
of loss, such as occurs in a love triangle. While envy is
always a sinful response, jealousy can be a legitimate
reaction to loss or the threat of loss. When another
person intrudes into a marriage, for example, jealousy is
an appropriate feeling. (Jealousy can be a pathological
reaction, however, when it is not based in reality.
Unfounded jealousy has been the destroyer of many
relationships.)

The kind of jealousy used to describe God in the
Bible refers to legitimate jealousy. When we read that
God is a jealous God, we are to understand that God
permits no rivals for our affection. We are to love him
first and foremost, with no other gods before him (Ex.

20:3–5). Here jealousy represents a protective aspect of intense and perfect love.

Envy, on the other hand, is the antithesis of love. In 1 Corinthians 13 we read that love "does not envy." Envy, in fact, prevents us from loving others, God, and even ourselves because we go through life feeling cheated. It is a magnet that attracts misery and discord in many forms. We can gain a better understanding of this destructive emotion by looking at envy's unsavory traveling companions. One or more of the following ten characteristics is a key component in any situation involving envy.

Greed. Desire is the first step of envy. When uncontrolled, desire becomes greed. As the greedy hunger and thirst for more and more, they look to what others possess to meet their own demands. Unfortunately, even that will never be enough. Isaiah 56:11 tells us that a mighty appetite is never satisfied.

Tolstoy told a story about a peasant that illustrates the extent of greed. The man was offered all the land he could walk around in one day. He covered such a tremendous territory that just as he returned at the end of the day, he fell dead from the great exertion. The end to his greed came only at his death.[2]

Self-Absorption. When we envy, we tend to place our needs and desires above those of our neighbor. We fix our eyes on ourselves and close them to others. When something good happens to someone else, we take it personally, as if she received a blessing only because it missed us. This side of envy has been noted by L. B. Flynn: "The envious man feels others' fortunes are his misfortunes; their profit, his loss; their blessing, his bane; their health, his illness; their promotion, his demotion; their success, his failure."[3]

Discontent. A lack of satisfaction with our position and possessions will cause us to focus on what others have. Grass is always greener on the other side when we have strewn the seeds of discontent on our side.

Judgmentalism. When we envy, we make a judgment that someone else has something that would better serve us. We develop a critical spirit as we decide who deserves what.

Fear. If we are anxious about tomorrow and fear that God will not provide our needs, we may envy the security we believe others have. Somehow we believe that God's provisions are limited and that what he gives to others will subtract from our own supply.

Insecurity. When we devalue ourselves, we believe we don't deserve what others have. Because we think we are not good enough to receive good things, we instead envy what others have.

Pride. Like envy, pride is comparative. It makes us want what others have so we can be better than they are. "Pride gets no pleasure out of having something, only out of having more of it than the next man," noted C. S. Lewis.[4]

Falsehood. When we envy, we may hide our true feelings under a mask of feigned delight at what others have. The loser of a beauty contest hugs the winner, with teeth gritted inside her smile. A child applauds her friend's report card, while secretly hating her for getting better grades. We may even try to convince ourselves that what others have is not worth having, as did the fox in the Aesop fable. When he tried to reach luscious, juicy grapes but repeatedly failed, the fox decided they were probably sour anyway. Envy sows dishonesty and keeps our relationships at a superficial level.

Bitterness. If we decide we can never attain what we envy, our envy may turn to bitterness. Envy is sustained only when the possibility exists that we can someday have what we want. For example, a child who envies a friend's height may become bitter once he reaches his full stature and realizes he will never grow taller.

Schadenfreude. This is a German word that stands for joy at another's suffering and pain at another's success. Envy separates us from the body of Christ and prevents us from fulfilling the exhortation in Romans 12:15: "Rejoice with those who rejoice; mourn with those who mourn."

ENVY: A COMPARATIVE CRISIS

Envy has its basis in comparison: we look at what we have and what others have and decide they have something we want. We want it so badly, in fact, that we feel angry they have it and we don't. We may even grow to hate those we envy. The hate may become so intense that it consumes us, as it did King Saul in his quest to destroy David.

A story from Jewish folklore illustrates the fervor of envy-induced hatred. One day an angel promised a businessman one wish. He could have whatever he wanted, provided his rival down the street received twice what was granted. The envious businessman immediately wished to be blind in one eye.

What drives us to hurt even ourselves in our envious crusade to keep another from besting us? What underlies our need to compare ourselves to others and come out on top? What causes us not only to envy, but also to want others to envy us?

The answer to these questions can be discovered through two more questions: Who am I? and Whose am I? We envy because we do not fully experience who we are and to whom we belong. We envy because we believe we need what another has and we will be little or nothing without it. Only as we realize the fullness of our life in Christ and in the body of Christ can we circumvent envy.

Who Am I?

When we don't know or like who we are, we spend our lives trying to be Someone Else. Someone Else listens to what others think Someone Else should be and takes their values as her own. Someone Else wants to look the way others think she should look. She wants to have what others think she should have, and she wants to do what others think she should do. Her warped sense of identity causes her to define herself in terms of her appearance, her possessions, and her accomplishments: Someone Else thinks that she is the sum of how she looks, what she owns, and what she does.

"I am how I look." It is particularly unfortunate that we place so much importance upon appearances. Our

106

culture seems to value women more for the size of their breasts than the size of their hearts. Wrinkles and bulges doom a woman to be devalued by society. Woe to anyone who has some body parts too big and others too small, eyes too close together or too far apart, or legs too short or too tall.

Parade magazine asked teenagers to respond to the question, "Does a person's different appearance affect the way you treat him or her?" One girl wrote that when she was fourteen years old, she contracted myasthenia gravis, a muscle disease that caused her eyelids to droop and her speech to slur. She said that before the disease she had many friends and was athletic, cheerful, and attractive, even winning beauty contests. After the disease, she wrote, "I lost more than my former appearance. I felt like I had lost my life. People shunned me. They made fun of me. *To others I was no longer the same person.* But all the time, I *was* the same person on the inside, longing to be treated the same as before."5

God, however, looks past our external appearances, straight through to our hearts (1 Sam. 16:7). Can you imagine how interesting life would be if we saw others inside-out, too? What a picture some would make if the size of their noses were determined by the bitterness in their hearts, if the length of their legs were determined by their eagerness to run to the aid of others, and if the smoothness of their skin were determined by their use of kind and gentle words.

As long as we place undue importance upon appearances, we will always find someone to envy. We need to remember that our bodies are basically houses for our spirit and will someday turn to dust. The prophet Isaiah told us that even Jesus had "no beauty or majesty to attract us to him, nothing in his appearance that we should desire him" (Isa. 53:2). While we can keep our vessels as clean and pleasant as possible, we certainly don't need to make them the center of our lives.

"I am what I own." We begin at a very young age to associate who we are with what we have. When a friend took her two-year-old shopping for new shoes, she was confused by the child's insistence to get "box." She thought her daughter wanted just the shoe box and not the shoes until the girl pointed to a pair of expensive Reeboks athletic shoes. Even though she had been talking and walking less than a year, the child already had been influenced by commercialism.

Somehow we believe that having the best makes us the best. We see celebrities and models hawking products in the media, and we believe that we can be like them if only we have what they have. We do well to recall the words of the prophet Jeremiah: "Does it make you a king to have more and more cedar?" (Jer. 22:15).

Cedar does not make someone a king any more than a certain fruit made Adam more like God. Things cannot bring happiness nor make us rich, beautiful people. Instead they can lead us away from the true values of life and consume us, as illustrated in the life of John D. Rockefeller, Sr. The world's only billionaire by age fifty-three, he was so ill from his attempts to control and protect his possessions that he could not sleep or eat anything other than crackers and milk. His health was restored only after he relaxed his grip on things and shared them with others.

"The bitterness, rancor and the deadness of self-centeredness went out of his life, and into the soul of John D. came refreshing streams of love and gratitude from those whom he was helping. He who had been repulsive and lifeless now teemed with vibrancy and activity," wrote S. I. McMillen, M.D., in *None of These Diseases*.[6]

If possessions say anything about who we are, they speak either about our generosity and selflessness or our greed and narcissism.

"I am what I do." We live in a culture that sizes people up by the job they do. Those who labor under cars or over greasy griddles are put in a separate category from those who work behind a desk. Even those who work at a desk are further stereotyped, depending upon whether they take dictation or give it. While both surgeons and mechanics work with their hands, one is white collar and one is blue collar.

We take so much identity from our jobs that some people would rather remain unemployed than do work they consider too unimportant, as did one young man who wrote to Ann Landers. Despite his failure to obtain a job in his field, he refused to work at a fast food restaurant for fear his college pals would see him there.

We don't seem to be able to get to know other people without placing them in the context of their job. The question we ask right after "Who are you?" is "What do you do?" We mentally determine whether another person's job is more or less prestigious than our own and whether it puts us in a one-up or one-down position. Those who do not work outside the home often feel embarrassed about their lack of a job, even when they are mothers who have chosen their families as their full-time careers. Those who have lost their jobs usually feel humiliation, even when they did nothing to cause their dismissal.

We can so strongly identify with what we do, that

when we don't do it, we don't know who we are. When the position ceases to exist, so does the person who filled it. That lack of identity outside work can lead to depression and suicide. A talented psychiatrist who lost his job during an administrative shake-up could not imagine life apart from his job. His response was to hang himself from the tree outside his former office.

While work can bring great meaning to our lives, it cannot be our reason for living. Even Solomon, the wisest man ever to live, recognized the limits of our careers. "I hated all the things I had toiled for under the sun, because I must leave them to the one who comes after me," he wrote in Ecclesiastes 2:18. While meaningful work is one of God's gifts to us, God never intended for us to worship it. When God put Adam in the Garden of Eden "to work it and take care of it," he never meant for Adam to obsess about his performance and take his identity from it (Gen. 2:15).

Whose Am I?

More than 130 times the New Testament tells us that as Christians, we are "in Christ." We belong to Christ because he bought us with his own blood. "You are not your own; you were bought at a price," Paul wrote to the Corinthians (1 Cor. 6:19–20).

Since we are in Christ, we are heir to all that he has—now and in our next life. In fact, the Bible tells us that God delights in satisfying us with good things (Ps. 103:5). If another person seems to have something good that we do not, we cannot put the blame on God. For a variety of reasons, we may not realize all of God's good gifts in this life, but we certainly will in the next. As we believe that God will never withhold anything good from us, we can put aside our envy and rejoice in knowing that God will work all things to our benefit.

Whenever we label the circumstances of our life "not good," we risk envy. We may decide that while our life is not good, the lives of others are good. Thus, we determine that God has favorites and showers others with more blessings than we get. If we look at the life of the apostle Paul, however, we can see that contentment actually has little to do with a good life. Paul, who experienced both plenty and need, learned contentment despite his circumstances. He trusted in God's sovereignty and accepted as a blessing both hardship and abundance, knowing that God was working all things to his benefit. Because Paul recognized that he belonged to Christ, he was secure in his circumstances, whatever they might be.

Not only do we belong to Christ, but each of us also belongs to the body of Christ (1 Cor. 12:27). All Christians comprise one entity, which has Christ at its head. What we do, think, or feel, therefore, affects not just us, but also the other members of the body, including Jesus. When we are generous to another Christian, that generosity touches the entire body.

Jesus tried to teach this concept to his disciples, pointing out that "whatever you did for one of the least of these brothers of mine, you did for me" (Matt. 25:40). Paul Maves has even suggested that our individual well-being is tied to the body: "There is no health in us as isolated individuals, but only in the wholeness of our corporate life when it exists as the Body of Christ," he wrote.[7]

A touching story that illustrates how the body of Christ should work concerns a boy named Jake, who lived in a poor orphanage with nine other young boys.[8]

At Christmas each boy received the rare treat of an orange. The orange was a prized possession. Each boy saved his orange for several days, admiring it, feeling it, loving it, and contemplating the moment he would eat it. Some would even save it until New Year's Day or later, as many of us leave out our Christmas trees and decorations just to remind us of the joy of Christmas.

This particular Christmas Day, Jake had broken the orphanage rules by starting a fight. The orphanage mother took Jake's orange as punishment. Jake spent Christmas Day empty and alone. Nighttime came and Jake could not sleep. Silently he sobbed because this year he would not have his orange to savor like the other boys.

Jake was startled when something was shoved into his hands by a boy who then disappeared into the dark. As he examined the hastily delivered gift, Jake discovered a strange-looking orange. It was an orange made from segments of the other nine oranges—nine coveted oranges that had to be eaten that Christmas night, instead of saved, admired, and cherished.

Giving, rather than envying, is what the body of Christ is all about. God calls each of us to participate in the creation of "strange-looking oranges" by regularly giving a part of ourselves to others. When we focus our attention on other people in need, envy disappears and caring emerges.

The body of Christ is difficult for us to fully comprehend in our individualistic society. At childhood our growth charts are compared, at school our grades, at puberty our pimples. When we think in terms of one another, it usually is in terms of competing, not completing. Yet completion is the task given to us by God; by fulfilling our part in the body, we make it perfect and

112

whole, just like the strange-looking orange. We cannot give to the body, however, if we are obsessed with taking from it.

MASTERING ENVY

Envy is a warning sign that all is not well with our soul. It is a spiritual cancer that will eat away at the contentment of our lives unless we determine to master it. Because the cure for envy lies in experiencing the fullness of our identity and position in Christ, here are six practical suggestions toward realizing who we are and whose we are.

1. Renew our image of God.

When we envy, we question the goodness of God. Our failure to realize that God is good and that he wills the best for our lives results in resentment against God and envy of others. We must remember that sin is responsible for our ills, not God.

"Whatever you *think* you lack is not God's fault. He willed the best for you because His love for you knows no limits," wrote Tony Campolo in *Seven Deadly Sins*. "What you have done, or what others have done, may have thwarted His will so that the good things He willed for you have not materialized; but remember, God is a good God who wills for you all of those gifts and attributes essential for you to live your life in the fullness of joy."[9]

We must see God as a fair and competent provider if we are ever to overcome envy.

2. Renew our self-image.

As we come to know God as a loving and providing Father, we will begin to recognize our value to him. Because God loves us, we have infinite value and purpose in his universe. Because his love is not based on our appearance, possessions, or performance, it will never be withdrawn or diminished. Thus, we have no need to envy those things in others, because they will not increase our stature or value before God.

Envy is a degrading emotion. When we envy, we are in effect saying, "I am not good enough without this or that." The more we feel good about who we are, the less we will feel a need to envy.

3. Get involved in the lives of others.

"If envy were not such a tearing thing to feel, it would be the most comic of sins. It is usually, if not always, based on a complete misunderstanding of another person's situation," wrote Monica Furlong in *Christian Uncertainties*.[10] If we were to walk a few moons in the moccasins of those we envy, we most likely would discover a craving for our own shoes. No one's life is as great as we imagine it to be. Whether rich or poor, famous or obscure, we all are real people with real hurts.

As we become involved in the lives of others, we discover they have needs just as we do. By focusing our attention upon others, we have less time and occasion for envy.

114

4. Find our place in the body of Christ.

God has called each of us to serve an important role in his universe. Until we find it, we may well envy others who seem to be a valuable part of God's kingdom. Indeed, we will not recognize our value in the body of Christ until we discover our place in it. To determine whether we are gifted at teaching, serving, praying, encouraging others, showing mercy, or any other gift, we can try out different roles to see what fits.

We err when we simply fill a vacancy or squeeze ourselves into what we consider an important role, like preaching or teaching. God never intended for us to envy one another's gifts in Christ; rather, he designed them to work together to make a perfect whole.

When we are content with our role, we free others to fulfill their positions in Christ. Like John the Baptist, we need to make room for others to minister. John easily could have become envious when his disciples told him that Jesus was baptizing and that "everyone [was] going to him" instead of John (John 3:26). Because John knew his role was to prepare the way for Christ, however, he was able to experience joy in his own role of diminishing prominence. If we look at what others do as a complement to our role, we will neither be threatened by their success nor envious of it.

5. Put possessions in their place.

A man who had been terrified to fly finally made his first anxiety-free flight. When asked how he handled it so calmly, he replied, "I never let my whole weight down."

That same perspective serves us well in the area of

possessions. We need to sit lightly on them, never letting down our whole weight. As we recognize that God is the owner and that we are just the caretakers, we develop a more carefree attitude toward the things of this world.

If things are too important in your life, one activity that can help break the power of your possessions is fasting. Just as fasting from meals can help us become less attached to this world and more spiritually attuned, so can fasting from things. For a period of time, fast from buying new things or fast from using certain things. If fasting from things is not enough, then give them away. When possessions possess you, they bring no pleasure.

6. *Evaluate our priorities.*

Envy offers a precise test of the condition of our heart. What do we envy? That is what we treasure.

God says our first priority should be his kingdom. If we truly concentrate on making God's desires our desires, then we have no room for envy. If we earnestly seek to be more loving, joyful, peaceful, patient, kind, good, faithful, gentle, and self-controlled, then we have no need of envy. Rather, we discover that God supplies these fruits of the Spirit in abundance to all who ask for them. We don't need to envy someone else's gentleness or patience because we have the same access to them. By changing our priorities from the things of the world to the things of God, we move into a realm where envy cannot follow.

NINE
When We Are Driven by the Orange Flames— Urgency

"Drive thy business," wrote Benjamin Franklin, "or it will drive thee."[1]

Today many of us know firsthand the truth of Franklin's warning. For us, life itself has become a business in which we plan our daily schedules as if they were profit and loss statements. With much to do in little time, we turn to time experts for advice on how to satisfy all the demands upon us.

Because we have been conditioned to equate success with busyness in our fast-paced, high-pressure culture, life on overdrive has become accepted rather than the exception. Unfortunately the constant pressure to do and be more results in a chronic feeling of urgency for many of us.

Although urgency is not an emotion per se, it can be seen as an orange flame arising from the commingling of fear (yellow) and anger (red). We *fear* we cannot keep up with life's demands and we become *angry* that we are subjected to them. The constant stress of living in this state of flight or fight brings with it all the ill effects associated with fear and anger.

THE HURRIED AND HARRIED LIFE

When life's demands take over the driver's seat, life becomes like the leech described in Proverbs 30:15 with two daughters who cry, "Give! Give!" No matter how much we do, it is never enough. We run out of hours before we meet all the demands on our time. Indeed, when *USA Today* tabulated the hours needed to satisfy "necessary" weekday activities, based on advice from various experts, it came up with a forty-two-hour weekday.[2] "With stopwatch in hand and tongue in cheek," the newspaper reported that an extra eighteen hours a day are necessary to fulfill our obligations for exercise, personal grooming, parenting, cooking, shopping, spiritual development, and other activities of import.

Weekends, once a time to recoup and slow down, have simply become stressful extensions of weekdays. What we don't get done during the week is pushed to Saturday and Sunday, noted a recent survey of weekend leisure time. "We've lost our weekend leisure time to an unending list of things to do," stated the report, which estimated the average adult spends fourteen weekend hours doing chores, running errands, and meeting other obligations.[3]

Our generation has witnessed the emergence of "pace addicts," psychiatrist Steven Fayer has explained. "A pace addict lives nonstop. She needs action, excitement, drama and intrigue—constant motion, in fact—to feel that her life is worth living. Her calendar is crammed full with appointments day and night for months ahead. The pace addict gets high from rushing through life. She just doesn't know how to stop."[4]

This time trap has been named "urgency addiction" by author Nina Tassi, who wrote that those suffering from this syndrome lose their inner sense of time.[5] Her research indicated that we escape this time warp only if we can be busy without being harried. "It is not a matter of being busy. . . . A person becomes a prisoner of time only when being busy yields to a pervasive sense of being harried," she suggested.

Tassi noted six traits common in those who are pressured by time. She said (1) they monitor time excessively, (2) they go at too fast a pace, (3) they work long hours, (4) they give up their own private time to others, (5) they lose the ability to enjoy the present moment, and (6) they postpone future goals and desires.

The Frenzied Christian

Christians especially seem prone to a hectic, crowded life, as noted by author Jean Fleming:

In the twenty some years I've been a Christian, I've received instruction on and been challenged to read my Bible daily, pray without ceasing, do in-depth Bible study regularly, memorize Scripture, meditate day and night, fellowship with other believers, always be ready to give an answer to the questioning unbeliever, give to missions and to the poor, work as unto the Lord, use my time judiciously, give thanks in all circumstances, serve the Body using my gifts to edify others, keep a clean house as a testimony, practice gracious hospitality, submit to my husband, love and train my children, disciple other women, manage finances as a good steward, involve myself in school and community activities, develop and maintain nonChristian friendships, stimulate my mind with careful read-

119

ing, improve my health through diet and exercise, color coordinate my wardrobe, watch my posture, and "simplify" my life by baking my own bread.[6]

The church, in fact, may even facilitate over-busyness, according to Tim Kimmel, president of Generation Ministries in Phoenix. "We demand that people be involved, and if you're not, your commitment and spirituality are in question," he said.[7] As Christians, we tend to justify our frantic pace because we are doing good things. Sometimes we forget that when our light shines, it burns, too.

The Bible has even been marketed for the busy Christian. Power Publications advertised that its KWIK-SCAN Bible enables a person to "read in just twenty minutes what normally takes you an hour to read."[8] *Reader's Digest* has also offered a condensed Bible.

Unfortunately, our rushed life may discourage others from the faith. Fleming noted that while her neighbors were drawn to her family, they rejected the gospel. "Their response was, 'We couldn't live at your pace.' They had been attracted to Christ, but the busyness of our lives had scared them from a commitment."[9]

God, however, has never called anyone to live at a hectic pace. Even renowned psychiatrist Carl Jung recognized the evil roots involved in the rushed life. "Hurry is not of the devil," he said. "It is the devil."[10]

The Toll of Urgency

An overscheduled life keeps us from scrutinizing and developing our values and goals, as well as our relationships with God and others. It results in an unexamined life, which Socrates admonished is a life not worth living. Indeed, when we rush through life, we substitute the shadow of life for the real thing. Our life becomes a thousand miles long and a millimeter deep.

Living nonstop also encourages us to rationalize our plight. To justify our hectic pace, we have redefined time in terms of quality and quantity. We don't have to worry about spending only a few minutes a day with our loved ones *if* we assure ourselves we have put in "quality time." Unfortunately, no amount of quality can make up for a lack of quantity. Our family and friends simply need our time. We do well to heed the warning that Pastor Alan Redpath displayed in his study at Moody Church: "Beware of the barrenness of a busy life."[11]

A constant feeling of urgency can also lead to burnout. Burnout, a reaction to chronic stress, is often the end product of a harried and hurried life. Ayala Pines and her colleagues have defined burnout as physical, mental, and emotional exhaustion that "usually does not occur as the result of one or two traumatic events but sneaks up through a general erosion of the spirit."[12]

With burnout comes the loss of your energy, the "e" of your emotions. Without this "e," your emotions become just motions. As Tassi noted, we lose the ability to feel or enjoy our activities. We behave as if we were on autopilot. We do rather than feel. We do rather than think. We do. We do. We do. Until one day, we wake up and we can't do anymore.

LIFE IN GOD'S REST

"If you experience stress, you're doing it wrong," Jay Conrad Levinson has suggested.[13] While we actually need a low level of stress in our lives to spur us to action, a high level of stress is destructive. It wars against our body, mind, and spirit with disastrous results. Researchers believe that too much stress can contribute to the onset of almost any physical or mental illness, as your body literally consumes itself in response to a physiologic overdrive. People experiencing excessive stress are even twice as likely to catch a cold.[14]

If we *are* doing it wrong, then, the question is, How do we do it right? How do we find the rest for our souls that Jesus promised in Matthew 11:28 when he said, "Come to me, all you who are weary and burdened, and I will give you rest"?

The answer is so simple that we often charge right by it in our frantic pace to complete our never-ending tasks. "Come to me," says Jesus. So simple, yet so challenging in a world that pulls and pushes. In order to meet our daily demands, we need our daily bread. We need the soul nourishment that comes from time with our Creator—the "be still" time that allows us to know God, not just to know about God (Ps. 46:10).

We need time to sit in God's presence, time to *be*, not to *do*. Not to do Bible study, not to do prayer requests, not to do Scripture memory. Time to simply enjoy God for who he is, not what he does, and to reflect on his Word. If you compare our relationship with God to our relationship with our loved ones, you can see that time spent constantly doing things together, without time for simply being together, would lead to a shallow and exhausting relationship.

We must be careful, however, not to categorize time with God as just one more thing to do. It is the *one* thing we do that enables us to do everything else. No matter how many things press in on us, we can take our example from Jesus, who faced unceasing pressures when he was on earth. So many to heal, so many to teach, so many to save. Yet we never read in the Bible, "Jesus hurried." Instead we see him regularly drawing away from the crowds and away from his disciples to spend time with his Father. For Jesus to accomplish his tasks on earth, he turned to God for strength and power. If Jesus needed this time, how can we pass it by?

Resisting God's Rest

Quiet time with God is probably the most difficult spiritual area for most Christians. We tend to do better with structured activities, such as serving on church committees, teaching Sunday school, and attending church and Bible studies. While our absence would be noted readily at those functions, no roll is called at our meetings with God. Unfortunately, we don't wear a scarlet A when we're absent from God's presence. Perhaps more of us would schedule regular meetings if we did.

Our neglect to spend time with God does show, however: in our impatience, our agitation, our irritability, and our weakness. Perhaps we fail to spend time with God because we fail to comprehend the strength and power available to us through him. We struggle on our own might, like a sparrow caught in a crosswind.

Yet we read in Isaiah 40:31 that when we hope in the Lord, he exchanges our weakness for his strength. It is at that point that we are able to "soar on wings like eagles." An eagle soars not by flapping and struggling, but by entering an updraft and being lifted on the wind. God is our updraft. When we strengthen our relationship with God through time with him, we more fully

123

experience his attributes, such as strength and power, in our own lives. Just as children assume the characteristics of those they are around the most, we too will be infused with God's attributes as we spend time with him.

Perhaps part of our negligence also stems from our propensity toward independence. The first sentence out of our infant mouths is, "I do it myself!" We strive so hard to make our own way in this world that we sometimes forget the owner of the path. We take off running without a look back until we find ourselves mired in a muddy trench or wounded by a falling rock.

Dependency has become a dirty word in our culture. No one wants to be known as a co-dependent, a label that carries all of the newest pathological implications. Yet in our haste to be our own person, we sometimes forget that we are *imago Dei,* or made in the image of God. We were created to find our fullness, our strength, and our culmination in God. Dependence upon God is not a crutch or an addiction; it is the completion of who we are.

Another excuse we often offer is busyness. We become so overwhelmed with squeaky wheels, situations that scream loudly for our time, that we have no time for God. It can be so easy to push aside God's gentle whisper while we race madly to and fro, trying desperately to oil all the squeaks. It is at this point that we need to reassess our attitude about life. What is important to us? Does our life reflect our values? Are we in control of our life, or are we tapping to the tune of a thousand different timekeepers?

We need to keep in mind, however, that busyness by itself is not the problem. In order to achieve God's rest, we don't have to retire from our careers to our corners, with Bible in one hand and meditation cap in the other. We don't have to become inactive. The Bible, in fact, is replete with admonitions to work wholeheartedly at whatever we do, and it compares the Christian life to a race. We only need to make sure that God isn't given our leftover time (if any). Our time with God must be a priority, a time of seeking his strength for our activities, his peace for our urgency, and his direction for our efforts.

RUNNING THE RACE BEFORE YOU

When our son was five years old he discovered, much to his delight, that he could outrace his mother across the hills of our backyard. With feet bare, eyes wide, and arms flailing, he ran with a certain recklessness that guaranteed our laughter and his victory. As he matures, however, Matthew will discover that winning races requires more than simply disabling your opponent. He will learn where to run, what to wear, and how to train.

The same principles for running that Matthew will learn can also be applied to our Christian life, which the apostle Paul often described as a race. We offer here nine guidelines toward helping us "run and not grow weary" (Isa. 40:31).

1. Choose our races carefully.

We are called to run the race before us—not every race. We don't need to serve on every committee, fight every evil, heal every wound, play in every game, and march in every parade. Even Jesus did not respond to every demand made of him. When he was asked to settle a question of inheritance, he replied, "Man, who appointed me a judge or an arbiter between you?" (Luke 12:14). Jesus knew the race before him, and he did not veer from its course.

Before we slip on our running shoes, we must decide what races are worth our life. If we want to choose the best races, we must be willing to take time for prayer and reflection. We need to ask, What am I trading my life for? Is it a "life worthy of the calling [I] have received" (Eph. 4:1)? Or is it a life of misdirected detours and spurious sprints, dictated by whatever demands pass our way?

We like to pass our priorities through the flammability test found in 1 Corinthians 3:13. There we read that on Judgment Day our work will pass through the fire and whatever is found unworthy will be burned up. This image became real for us when we witnessed a "flammability preview" shortly after we moved from our dream home. On the eastern shore of Maryland, it was a three-story, 104-year-old Victorian mansion that we had lovingly and meticulously restored. We had jacked up floors, torn out walls, scraped multiple layers of paint, installed new appliances, and had it replumbed, rewired, and reroofed. When we sold it and moved to another state a few years later, we felt that we had left behind a part of us.

Then we heard that it had burned to the ground. Our dream home was now a parking lot for the funeral home next to it. Suddenly the things of this world showed themselves for their true nature—fleeting. Gone in an instant.

Our heartfelt recognition of the temporal nature of things doesn't mean that we don't enjoy them. It just means that we try to keep them in perspective and use them in a way that furthers God's kingdom on earth. We push them to the side of our races while we remind ourselves of what has eternal value—God's people and God's Word.

This experience has taught us to question how much of our struggle and labor is for naught, never to pass from this life to the next. It has helped us to focus on these questions as we make decisions concerning the races we choose: Is this something that will make me more Christlike? Will it further God's kingdom in my life and the lives of others? Will it enable me to share God's love and healing with others? Will it create joy and peace in my life? If we cannot answer yes to these four questions, then we may need to choose a better race.

2. Stay in our lane.

Once we have marked our course, we must be willing to say no to whatever distracts us from our chosen races. Saying no becomes easier when we realize that every time we say yes to something, we are effectively saying no to something else. When we agree to serve on yet another committee, we are also agreeing to cut back on the time we spend with our family. When we consent to work overtime, we also consent to enjoy less time for rest and relaxation.

3. Wait for the starting gun.

False starts have been the downfall of many good runners. Waiting is never easy, whether in a real race or in our Christian walk. Perhaps that is why we are repeatedly admonished in the Bible to wait for God, for his starting signal. Our tendency is to jump out of the blocks and sprint to the finish. We often opt for Thomas Edison's quip: "Everything comes to him who hustles while he waits."[15]

We often act first and pray about it later. "By the way, God," we might say, "as long as I'm in the middle of this project, do you mind blessing it?" Because God's timing is perfect, however, we quickly discover that a race run before its time is a wasted race. Until we are sure of God's timing, we do better to wait.

4. Focus on one step at a time.

Mark Porter told of the time a high school junior, John Baker, ran his first cross-country race. To everyone's surprise, Baker defeated the state champion and set a new record. Porter reported that Baker won the race because "he focused on the runner in front of him, and set as his goal passing that runner. He shut out of his consciousness the overall goal of winning the race."[16]

We can benefit from Baker's technique, too. When life becomes overwhelming, we need to focus on one step at a time, not the finish line. This is a difficult task for many of us. We have a hard time thinking about what we *are* doing without fretting about what we are *not* doing. We tend to think about the mountain of laundry while we are changing diapers, and about our next sales prospect before we have wrapped up the current deal. This diluted focus, however, robs us of enjoyment of the present and makes us anxious about the future.

We once had a dog who could focus on one thing at a time better than anyone else. We would set out a treat for Brandy, only to make her wait to eat it until we

128

snapped our fingers. The way she kept herself from a premature lunge at the food was to look only at us while she waited for her signal. Had Brandy peeked at the treat, she would never have been able to exercise such self-control.

We find that same focus works for us, too. When our "to do" list seems longer than *War and Peace,* we stay focused on the task at hand by keeping other projects out of mind and often out of sight. We keep our eyes and thoughts on what we're doing now, just like our dog kept her eyes on us. This means keeping desks cleared of anything that won't be tackled today. Not making a detailed study of the green mold in the refrigerator. Learning to look past the table that cries for Pledge. Not allowing our mind to wander forward into the marsh of tomorrow. We tattoo Ecclesiastes 3:1 upon our foreheads: "There is a time for everything, and a season for every activity under heaven." When the thought of another task tries to force its way into our brain, we push it away with the reprimand, "This is not your time!"

We need to remember that the problem isn't always the multitude of our activities; it is the *thinking* about all our activities. We have to learn to mentally dump tomorrow's tasks back into the job jar and then tighten the lid.

5. Eliminate excess weight.

Even the fittest runner might never finish a race were he to wear a one-hundred-pound backpack and ten-pound leg weights. Instead runners strip to the barest essentials. Yet many of us try to run the race of life while dragging excess baggage that makes us work all the harder.

How many things are you hauling through this life? Sometimes we confuse Jesus' promise to give us abundant joy with abundant possessions. Perhaps much of what we own is not a blessing from God, but a curse from Satan that distracts us from running the best race. As Henry David Thoreau lamented, "We now no longer camp as for a night, but have settled down on earth and forgotten heaven."[17]

How much time do you spend shining, oiling, watching, storing, dusting, cleaning, repairing, organizing, and showing off your possessions? Most of us underestimate just how much we have and overestimate how much others have. (Imelda Marcos did not have three thousand pairs of shoes. "I had one thousand and sixty," she pointed out.[18])

Whether our weakness is shoes, books, or gadgets, we need to take inventory of our possessions at least yearly and give away what is weighing us down, either in terms of our time, space, finances, or spiritual growth. "That which you cannot give away, you do not possess," suggested Ivern Ball. "It possesses you."[19]

6. Know our pace.

In his first ten-mile race, Mark watched as two other rookie runners galloped off into the distance far ahead of the pack. He didn't see them again until they were being placed into the ambulance, suffering from heat stroke. In not knowing their pace, they exceeded it.

We all have our own pace. Some people need only five hours of sleep a night, while others need twice that. Some thrive on schedules that would put their friends in the hospital for exhaustion. Some of us talk faster than others can listen.

Whether we sprint, jog, or stroll through life, however, we need to set our pace based on what is right for us, not someone else. We have a tendency to think that we should all be sprinters, that those who set a slower pace are somehow not running as fast as they should. Instead we should respect those who know their limits, pace themselves, and finish the race without collapsing from fatigue. We must realize the truth of poet John Milton's words: "They also serve who only stand and wait."[20]

7. Air out our running shoes.

"There cannot be a crisis next week," Henry Kissinger once said. "My schedule is already full."[21]

Some of us understand his chagrin only too well. Our appointment calendars are booked well into eternity. We can't air out our running shoes because we are wearing them all the time. Unfortunately we may end up not only with stinky feet, but also with a stinky life. We risk becoming like the man who wrote his own epitaph: "Born—a human being; died—a wholesale grocer."[22] The man regretfully explained that he was so busy making a living that he never had time to live.

We need some time for doing nothing every day, without feeling guilty about it. When we zealously schedule every minute with activities and then dash through the day as if it were a track meet, people can get lost. "I can't program people into my life the way I can writing," wrote Marlene LeFever, a self-confessed recovering time-management junkie. "People are messier. Their friendships and their needs often run into other time slots and mess up my whole day's plan."[23]

If you feel guilty leaving white space on your

calendar, pencil in AOT, for "air-out time," and think about 2 Corinthians 2:14. That verse reminds us that we are to be the fragrance of Christ to others, an impossible task when our feet are stinking.

When we leave empty time in our day, it allows God to use us where we have not planned it, to fill those hours with his purposes. If Moses had been running at our pace, would he have seen the burning bush? How many opportunities to hear God have we missed because of our production schedule? How much of heaven have we missed on earth? We can profit from Elizabeth Barrett Browning's words: "Earth's crammed with heaven, And every common bush afire with God; but only he who sees takes off his shoes; the rest sit round it and pluck blackberries."[24]

If your sneakers haven't been aired for a long time, you need to determine why you can't take them off. Are you too busy because you are trying to please others, who admire all that you do? Are you sheltering yourself from troubled relationships by being too busy to deal with problems? Are you avoiding negative feelings, such as guilt or envy? Are you trying to avoid other responsibilities? Are you discontent with what you have? Are you doing everything yourself because no one else does it well enough to please you? Do you believe that you are indispensable? Do you have to have everything just right? Until you understand why you need to run constantly, you will make no real progress toward airing out your running shoes.

8. Train faithfully.

Paavo Nurmi, known as the Flying Finn, ran seven races in six days in the 1924 Olympics. After Nurmi won the 1,500-meter and 5,000-meter events, his friends saw him on his way to a celebration party in Paris—walking the six miles instead of joining them on the bus! Nurmi continued to walk at least eight miles a day until he died, even though he suffered in later years from partial paralysis on his left side and blindness in his left eye. His discipline helped him become one of the greatest long-distance runners in history.

Christians can also benefit from the strict training practiced by runners, advised the apostle Paul. "They do it to get a crown that will not last; but we do it to get a crown that will last forever," he wrote to the Corinthians (1 Cor. 9:26). When we discipline ourselves to put God's kingdom first in our life, we realize a crown of spiritual blessings that begins in this world and lasts for eternity.

Such discipline is not always easy in our society. "Precisely because our secular milieu offers us so few spiritual disciplines, we have to develop our own. We have, indeed, to fashion our own desert where we can withdraw every day, shake off our compulsions, and dwell in the gentle healing presence of our Lord," wrote Henri J. M. Nouwen.[25]

Such discipline is also most difficult in its early stages, when we spend time with God primarily because we should. As we grow in our relationship with him, however, we find that desire replaces obligation. "A true love to [God] shall make this duty easy," wrote François Fenelon.[26] In the meantime, we can profit from Mark Twain's advice: "Make it a point to do something every day that you don't want to do. This is the golden rule for acquiring the habit of doing your duty without pain."[27] When we make it a point to sacrifice a portion of our time to God every day, at some point we discover it is no longer a sacrifice.

9. *Monitor our hearts.*

Serious athletes monitor their hearts. They know that if their pulse is too slow, their heart will not get a sufficient workout. If it is too fast, their heart will be overworked. As Christians, we also need to keep close tabs on our hearts, measuring the effect of our running.

"Is my heart in stable condition?" is a question we need to ask on a regular basis. Judy Seabaugh suggested that busyness can cause our heart to become like the inn that did not have room for the Son of God to be born.[28] We need to keep our hearts in "stable condition," she wrote, so that we, like the stable of Jesus' birth, have room for Jesus. "Am I so filled with the cares of life, stress, busyness and selfish desires that no room is left in my heart for Jesus?" she asked.

The busier we are, the more room we should make for God. Martin Luther used to explain that because he had so much to do, he needed at least three hours daily in prayer or "the devil gets the victory through the day."[29] A good rule of thumb for judging our busyness is to do no more than we can pray over.

Even when we regularly work at keeping our hearts in stable condition, we will find ourselves racing at times and out of breath. We all experience periods when we are overwhelmed with too much to do, such as when a child is ill or work deadlines are upon us. Even Jesus was so busy at times that he missed meals. "Spiritual breathing" can be a help to us then. First we simply relax for a minute and close our eyes. Then we breathe out our frustrations, worries, and woes, and breathe in the Spirit of God. These minute vacations with God help redirect our focus, settle our anxieties, and bring our hearts back to stable condition.

Keeping our hearts in stable condition also requires us to make sure our hearts are getting enough of a workout. We can't expect our hearts to carry us through tough races unless they first have been strengthened with regular workouts. "You cannot suddenly fabricate foundations of strength; they must have been building all along," wrote Philip Yancey.[30] Only when we spend time allowing God to condition our hearts can we be confident of running without growing weary.

TEN

When Black Darkens Our World—Guilt

There was a young lady of crime
Who felt guilty all of the time,
'Til she discovered a shrink
Who taught a new way to think;
She still steals but now feels sublime!

Our limerick points out the central principle of guilt: being guilty and feeling guilty are two entirely different matters. While therapists and counselors may help rid us of guilt feelings, they can do nothing about our actual guilt. On the other hand, many of us who have been released from the fact of guilt still suffer terribly from feelings of guilt. To handle guilt effectively, then, we must deal with both its fact and its feeling.

THE FACT OF GUILT

The Bible speaks clearly to the fact of our guilt: we are all sinners, and the wages of our sin is death. "If we claim to be without sin," says 1 John 1:8, "we deceive ourselves and the truth is not in us." Unfortunately the subject of sin has become an unmentionable in today's culture, as pointed out by *The Wall Street Journal:* "Moral judgments aren't made much anymore, especially not in print or on TV. Among intellectuals and commentators, judgment was long ago replaced by therapy. Ministers and priests gave way to clinics and counselors."[1]

As a result, people today have a hard time accepting the fact of their guilt. "People are no longer sinful, they are only immature or underprivileged or frightened or, more particularly, sick," noted American poet Phyllis McGinley.[2] It is far more comforting to believe that we are born good and strive to be good in a dysfunctional world that is evil. Christianity does not begin in comfort, however, explained C. S. Lewis in *Mere Christianity*. It begins in dismay.

"Christianity tells people to repent and promises them forgiveness. It therefore has nothing (as far as I know) to say to people who do not know they have done anything to repent of and who do not feel that they need any forgiveness. It is after you have realized that there is a real Moral Law, and a Power behind the law, and that you have broken that law and put yourself in wrong with the Power—that Christianity begins to talk," Lewis wrote.[3]

Once we allow Christianity to talk to us about our guilt, we find that it has a great deal to say about our forgiveness. The entire emphasis of Scripture is on forgiveness, with at least sixty references to it in the New Testament and even more in the Old Testament. The root meaning of forgiveness in both Hebrew and Greek is "to send away": God deals with the fact of our guilt by sending away its cause—our sin. God does not overlook sin, excuse it, or forget about it. Our sin must be sent away. Until we are willing to have our sin sent away through the blood sacrifice made by Jesus Christ, our sin and guilt remain with us.

THE FEELINGS OF GUILT

While God's forgiveness sends away the fact of guilt, it does not send away the feelings of guilt. False guilt is a common problem for many Christians who, despite being set free, still live in the blackness of their sins. Living in a world darkened by guilt causes a variety of disastrous effects for the person who is forgiven but doesn't live like it.

Jean was one such Christian. Two years ago she had an affair that nearly cost her marriage. Despite asking for forgiveness from both God and her husband, she still felt so guilty that she quit attending church. She suffered from constant headaches and lived in terror that God would punish her by taking the life of her child. Because she believed she no longer deserved her husband's love, she had emotionally withdrawn from their marriage. Thoughts of her betrayal consumed her. She didn't understand why she had done such a terrible thing, nor how she could ever be forgiven. "If God has really forgiven me, then why does he constantly bring my sin before me?" she asked when they came for marital counseling.

Three common misperceptions about guilt were evident in Jean's thinking: (1) she believed she needed to pay for her sin, (2) she thought her sin made her less valuable, and (3) she confused feelings of guilt for feelings of conviction.

Because Jean did not feel forgiven for her sin, she was trying to pay for it by punishing herself. Jean had to recognize her self-destructive behavior and its effect upon her physical health and her marriage. She had to understand that she could never do what Christ has already done: pay the debt of her sin.

Jean also had to realize that ever since she had become a Christian, she had been trying to earn her own righteousness before God. She believed that God would love her only if she were good enough. Every time she did a good work, she mentally added another stripe to her sleeve. Therefore, when she fell, she felt demoted and devalued. Because she had believed that her worth was based on her goodness, she had nothing on which to base God's love. Jean had to learn that no one has ever earned God's love, that we all fall short, that if she were perfect, she would not be human. She had to see herself through God's eyes, as someone with infinite value created in God's image.

Jean also had to be taught the difference between guilt feelings and conviction. Both concern our failings, but there the similarity ends. Guilt feelings are destructive; they are generated through our conscience; they address only confessed sin; and they result in more darkness. Conviction, on the other hand, is redemptive; it comes from the Holy Spirit; it addresses specific, unconfessed sin; and it is designed to bring about repentance and light.

God was no longer convicting Jean of her unfaithfulness. That sin had been sent away long ago when she had asked for forgiveness. The Holy Spirit never convicts us of confessed sin; in fact he doesn't even remember it. Therefore, whenever we are plagued by guilt about sin we have confessed, we can be assured that God has nothing to do with our feelings. The Bible reminds us that Satan, not God, is our accuser.

When the Holy Spirit convicts us of sin, it is always something we have yet to deal with. He brings to mind attitudes and behaviors that interfere in our relationship with God and others. The sole purpose of his conviction is to lead us to repentance and joy, not to guilty feelings.

LIVING IN A DARKENED WORLD

What happens when we, like Jean, are forgiven yet do not live in God's forgiveness? Then we must find ways to deal with our guilt feelings. Like Jean, we may try to pay for it ourselves. Or we may try to deny it, or we may simply succumb to it. Unfortunately, none of these coping strategies resolve guilt feelings. And while they may be used by both Christians and non-Christians, our remarks here are directed to those whom God has forgiven but who have difficulty accepting it.

Paying for Our Guilt

When we don't claim the sacrifice that Jesus made, our feelings of guilt may cause us to sacrifice ourselves. We then engage in moral masochism, in which we feel a need to suffer as payment for our sins. People suffering from guilty feelings often punish themselves through self-destructive behavior that can range from substance abuse to suicide. Like Jean, they even may make themselves sick. Dr. David Belgum has suggested that when we punish ourselves with illness, our physical symptoms are actually involuntary confessions of guilt.[4]

Another way we may try to pay for our guilt is by collecting the payment from someone else. If we don't understand that Jesus paid our debt of guilt, we may try to squeeze it from someone in our debt. A mother may

lose her temper with her children and blame them for
her anger: "If you weren't such rotten kids I wouldn't
have to scream at you. You drive me to it." When we
don't feel forgiven from our guilt, we have difficulty
forgiving our own debtors their debts.

Some of us may also try to pay for our sins through
our own goodness, as if we could reimburse God. With
guilt as our motivator, we seek our own self-righteous-
ness. Our quest leads us to become perfectionists at
whatever we do, whether it is teaching Sunday school or
trying to "win" converts. With each accomplishment,
we add another notch to the belt that holds in our guilt.
When we fall, however, we lose our sense of worth. We
also fail to realize that in trying to earn our forgiveness,
we take away from what Christ alone can do.

Denying Our Guilt

We may rationalize our sin in our efforts to escape
feelings of guilt. We find excuses for our behavior,
believing that a good reason exempts us from guilt.
"Well, I may have been unfaithful to my husband, but
he is cold and distant to me. I needed to feel appreciated and loved," a wife may explain. When we deny our
guilt, however, we deny our need for pardon and limit
God's forgiveness.

In denying our guilt, we often compare our behavior to others', ranking our own sin as less significant.
Some churches even encourage such beliefs by focusing
on certain external sins, like divorce or drunkenness. As
a result, we may believe that because we refrain from
certain behaviors we are somehow less guilty than
others. This kind of thinking, however, ignores the
warning given in James 2:10: "Whoever keeps the

141

whole law and yet stumbles at just one point is guilty of breaking all of it." God doesn't keep a list of "great," "moderate," and "tiny" sinners. Sin is sin, and we all are guilty.

Succumbing to Our Guilt

Guilty feelings may also cause just the opposite reaction: we see the futility of ever measuring up to God's standards and give up trying. In deciding that we are too far from forgiveness to ever reach it, we become the victims of our feelings. Our guilt keeps us stuck to the church pews because we feel too unworthy to serve. Even if we believe we will make heaven (through the back gate), we decide we are too wicked to offer anything of value here on earth.

Les Carter told of one woman who was so sure that she would never earn her way into heaven that she made small fires in her yard. Holding her hands as close to the fire as she could bear, she tried to prepare herself for the flames of hell. Her feelings of guilt led her to believe she could never know God's forgiveness.[5]

Some of us who believe we can never measure up not only stop trying to reach God, but we also actively run from him. Rebelling against what we consider to be an impossible goal, we allow our guilt to drive us to sin. We find an aberrant form of security in our belief that the more we sin, the more we can be assured of God's unwillingness to forgive us. Thus we are relieved from a futile effort to be forgiven.

However we try to cope with our guilt feelings outside of God's forgiveness, we fail. In order to resolve our feelings of guilt, we must send them away. Just as the fact of God's forgiveness sends away the fact of our

142

guilt, our feeling of God's forgiveness will send away feelings of guilt. It is not enough to know we are forgiven; we must feel we are forgiven. Forgiveness must penetrate our emotions. To remove the blackness of guilt feelings, our knowledge of forgiveness must reach from our head to our heart. That transmittal requires us to bring our feelings of guilt into God's light.

BRINGING LIGHT INTO OUR DARKENED WORLD

Ridding ourselves of guilt feelings is a process of illumination. It doesn't happen with the flick of a light switch; we can't send away our feelings via Federal Express. For change to occur, we have to be willing both to think about our guilt feelings and to invest time and energy in the process. As you reflect on the following five concepts, keep in mind that their value is dependent upon how real they become in your life. Although change is always a challenge, the result of moving from the darkness of guilt into the light of God's forgiveness is well worth the effort.

1. Our relationship with God is reflected, not established, by obedience.

When we realize that our relationship with God is not dependent upon how well we follow his commands, we are freed to admit our guilt. We know that we belong to God and that our disobedience will not cause him to reject us. This sense of security is the springboard to our acknowledgment of sin. As John Calvin wrote, "A man cannot apply himself seriously to repentance without knowing himself to belong to God."[6]

We must also understand that no one except God is good and that even our desire to be good is not self-generated but is given to us by God (Rom. 3:10–11). To be human is to be imperfect, in need of God's bountiful mercy. If our relationship with God depended upon our obedience, we would be without hope.

Instead, our desire to obey flows from our relationship with God. It is a reflection of the depth of our relationship. The closer we become to God, the better we become at obeying him.

We need to remember, however, that relationships take time to develop. When we become Christians, we don't suddenly find ourselves in tune with God and his values for us. While our spirit has been regenerated, our mind has not. We retain our old thought patterns, emotional responses, and selfish desires. Unless we actively work at developing our relationship with God, our new nature will not grow. Our spiritual development does not occur naturally alongside our physical development. Because growth indicates life, however, we should expect progress in our relationship with God, even though it may be uneven. "We know that we have come to know him," wrote the apostle John, "if we obey his commands" (1 John 2:3).

Obedience demonstrates our love for God; it does nothing to earn it.

2. Our conscience should not always be our guide.

"Let your conscience be your guide," was one of Jiminy Cricket's favorite lines. It may be good advice for bugs, who have no Spirit to guide them. We human beings, however, need to be wise to the problems our conscience can create.

144

Our conscience holds our internalized set of values, expectations, rules, and moral codes. When it has been developed in a healthy and godly fashion, it serves us well. The Bible therefore emphasizes the importance of training our children in holiness and love: we are helping to form their conscience.

A conscience can also be badly programmed through parental neglect or overindulgence, poor peer modeling, societal prejudice, and experiences with abuse, hatred, or rejection. Scripture paints a sordid picture of such a conscience as unreliable, weak, unsuitable, and even seared.

Thankfully, when we become Christians, our conscience is enlightened by the Holy Spirit, making it open to a new way of thinking. Unfortunately, however, it retains its earlier programming. Our conscience becomes re-programmed only as we input the values and morals of God. We have to be discerning, therefore, whenever our conscience condemns us and remember that the Holy Spirit's conviction always concerns an unconfessed sin. When our conscience targets confessed sin, we can circumvent the guilt feelings by reminding ourselves of the forgiveness already given us by God, who is greater than our conscience (1 John 3:20).

3. Sin is more terrible than we can know.

Our society has a particularly flippant attitude toward sin. We tend to excuse and overlook it because we have seen so much of it, particularly in the news and entertainment industries. Because we have come to expect it as the product of a dysfunctional environment, sin rarely shocks us anymore, save for particularly gruesome or violent acts.

As a result, we have lost sight of the seriousness of sin and the separation it has created between us and our Creator. When we fail to comprehend the gravity of sin, we fool ourselves into thinking that we can somehow justify ourselves before God by our own efforts. Our repentance becomes superficial when we accept God's forgiveness without knowing how our sin affects God. Our gratitude for our salvation becomes meaningless when we fail to understand the price God paid for our sin.

4. God loves us more than we can know.

Our image of God is key to our ability to feel forgiven. If we believe that God grants our forgiveness grudgingly and would just as soon swat us as save us, we will be unable to freely accept his forgiveness. We will always believe we are in God's debt, and we will always feel guilty about that debt.

We need to remember that our image of God may be distorted, especially if we have grown up under the rule of a cold, distant, or abusive parent. David Heller has reported that family imagery strongly influences deity imagery—we tend to see God in terms of our earthly parents.[7] A distorted image of God prevents us from understanding our value to God. It prevents us from knowing that God forgives us because we are worth forgiving and that our worth to God is based not on our merit but on God's love. Not until we see a loving Father will we be able to see a child worth saving. We must feel worthy of God's forgiveness before we can freely accept it.

146

5. *Repentance keeps us living in God's forgiveness.*

When we repent of our sins as the Holy Spirit brings them before us, we allow God to breathe life into our souls. We exhale sin and inhale forgiveness, which is a vital form of mouth-to-mouth resuscitation for the Christian.

Repentance starts with confession, which is more than just admitting to a specific sin. Its literal meaning is "to say the same as." To confess a sin is to agree with God about it, to take God's side in hating it.

Once we have confessed our sin, we need to repent of it. Repent is a military term that means "about face." When we repent, we change the direction of our life. We start over, ready to march away from our sin.

Every time you repent, you can be assured that God has forgiven you—even if you don't feel forgiven. As you work through your feelings of guilt, however, you will begin to feel God's forgiveness and to experience the freedom and life that repentance brings. Whatever feelings of guilt remain, draw in a fresh breath of forgiveness and blow the guilt feelings away. They have no rightful place in the life of any Christian.

ELEVEN

Living in the Pink

While research is abundant on why people get sick (pathogenesis), much less is available on why people stay well (salutogenesis). Even the definition of what comprises emotional health is a source of controversy. Some suggest it is the absence of ailments, putting us in the pink whenever we are not seeing red, feeling blue, or turning green. Others suggest it results from a way of looking at life that transcends feelings. Still others define well-being in terms of successful coping mechanisms: when we deal effectively with negative emotions, we reap positive feelings.

Positive emotions themselves have been singularly ignored or de-emphasized historically. Our language has more labels for negative emotions than positive, and we also use more negative facial expressions.[1] We seem to know a lot more about feeling bad than feeling good.

Perhaps part of the problem stems from confusion over the value of good feelings. Does happiness make us healthy, as advised by some? Or is it "detrimental to other valued things [because] it turns people into contented cows and it undermines social bonds," as suggested by others?[2]

148

We believe that emotions themselves cannot be blamed or commended for anyone's state of being. Instead their value for Christians can be determined by the spiritual growth they produce in us. When we experience an unpleasant feeling such as sadness, we may turn away from God or we may draw closer to him. Likewise when we experience a pleasant feeling such as happiness, we may forget about God or we may become more like him.

For the Christian, spiritual wellness must take precedence over emotional wellness, as Vernon C. Grounds pointed out: "An individual, quite completely free from tension, anxiety, and conflict, may be only a well-adjusted sinner who is dangerously maladjusted to God; and it is infinitely better to be a neurotic saint than a healthy-minded sinner."[3] As evidenced in the life of the apostle Paul and many Christians since, God most often works through our weaknesses, whether they are emotional or physical, instead of simply eliminating them.

Living in the pink, then, is not a matter of eluding negative feelings or pursuing positive ones. Our well-being is instead dependent upon growing through our feelings to become more like God, in whose image we were created. Whether we are seeing red or feeling blue, we can remain in the pink as long as we use our feelings to bring us closer to God.

Historically, this "cure of the soul" was the focus of healing. Only since the growth of science and the decline of religion has mind wellness superseded and even replaced soul wellness. Despite psychotherapy's attempts to distance itself from soul cure, however, many of today's mental health professionals have again moved toward helping people with spiritual struggles.[4]

Arthur Kornhaber, a nationally known child psychiatrist, often brings prayer into his sessions. "To exclude God from psychiatric consultation is a form of malpractice for some patients," Kornhaber said. "Spirituality is wonder and joy, and shouldn't be left in the clinical closet."[5]

Carl Jung noted that "patients force the psychotherapist into the role of the priest.... That is why we psychotherapists must occupy ourselves with problems which strictly speaking belong to the theologian."[6] When "properly understood, psychotherapy is in essence a spiritual process," suggested David G. Brenner.[7]

If wholeness concerns our state of spirit as well as our state of mind, then negative emotions can be as important as positive emotions. This has profound implications for Christian counseling. "It means that there are times when we ought to look at our psychological problems as part of the providential ordering of our lives by God," wrote C. Stephen Evans. "There are times when the proper goal of the Christian counselor is not the elimination of a problem but is helping an individual discover how a problem can be the occasion for spiritual growth."[8]

Too often, however, we try to eliminate emotional discomfort as quickly as possible. We try to deny it, drown it in alcohol or drugs, or dump it on somebody else. Whenever we try to lose, instead of use, negative emotions, we miss an opportunity to grow.

THE FOUNDATION FOR EMOTIONAL HEALTH

While psychologists may define emotional well-being quite differently, they have reached some agreement upon what makes us healthy. At the heart of our well-being, they say, is the satisfaction of four basic needs: identity, belonging, competence, and significance.

Interestingly, these same needs are addressed in the Bible. God puts them forth as four direct questions: "Where are you?" "Where is your brother?" "What is that in your hand?" "What are you doing here?" As we examine his inquiries, we must determine our own answers to each one. Keep in mind that your responses affect your capacity to use your emotions for growth and thus your ability to live in the pink.

Where Are You? Our Need for Identity

In Genesis 3:9 we read that "the Lord God called to the man, 'Where are you?'" God, of course, had not lost the man and woman he had created in his image. He knew where Adam and Eve were hiding, and he knew why. Because they had rejected God's image in themselves and had chosen to go their own way, Adam and Eve had been separated from God. At that point they discovered they were naked, or stripped of their identity with God. They knew they were alone, and they were afraid.

As a result of sin, we too suffer from this damaged sense of identity. Sin has forced us to come into the world incomplete, with a God-shaped vacuum in our hearts. Even though this void is meant to be filled by God, we so often pour other things into it that we cease to feel the lack of God in our lives. We may fill it with education, friendships, and even good works, but if our search for self is in isolation from God, it is merely a quest for self-fulfillment and not self-discovery.[9] Unless

151

God fills our void with himself, we may sense satisfaction in life, but we retain a warped sense of identity.

Despite being born broken, we, like Adam and Eve, hide from the Master Fixer. It is not we who seek God; it is God who calls to us, "Where are you?" God longs to restore his image in us. And because we are image-bearers of God, our wholeness depends upon our oneness with him. Without our identity in God, we will forever struggle to know ourselves apart from him, despite how satisfied we may feel with our life.

Where Is Your Brother? Our Need for Belonging

While God's first question concerns our relationship with him, his second question concerns our relationship with others. In Genesis 4:9 we read that Cain murdered his brother Abel and then had to answer to God, who asked, "Where is your brother?" Cain's infamous defense was that he was not his brother's keeper.

Although Cain may not have been his brother's keeper, he certainly was his brother's brother, suggested Ruth Bell Graham, who pointed out that while zoos, bees, and prisons have keepers, "only families have brothers."[10] God created us not to live as solitary creatures, but in relationship with others. "It is not good for the man to be alone," God said in Genesis 2:18. Christianity is a corporate concept—we are called to be part of the body of Christ.

God created us not just to belong to him, but also to belong to others. Eric L. Johnson has termed this a trialectical dynamic, which is a reciprocal relationship between three poles: God, ourselves, and others.[11] John H. Westerhoff described the effect of this connection:

"Our created corporate selfhood places us in an essential relationship with *all* others. Because God is in relationship with all persons, we cannot be in full community with God unless we also identify with and seek the good of *all* persons.[12]

Our very identity is bound up in relationships. We are born physically out of the relationship of our parents, and we are born spiritually out of the relationship of the Godhead. Our need for relationships is so strong that total isolation is almost always an intolerable situation for the human adult. Some theorists postulate that our need for meaningful relationships is biologically, and not just socially, based.[13]

God intended for our relationships on earth to mirror our relationship with him. Because of sin, however, the intimacy, love, and belonging that we experience with others is a dim reflection of what we will perfectly experience with God in heaven. It is this imperfect sense of belonging to others, however, that helps us to understand how we belong to God. People who have realized little sense of belonging to others often experience difficulty in believing that they belong to God.

What Is That in Your Hand?
Our Need for Competence

When God called Moses to free the Israelites, Moses told God he was inadequate for the task. He said he was afraid that the Egyptians would not believe that he had been sent by God. In Exodus 4:2 we read that God responded to Moses' inadequacies with a question: "What is that in your hand?" When Moses answered that it was a staff, God turned it into a snake.

Like Moses, we may feel that our hands have little to offer. Like Moses, we may forget that our competence comes from God, that it is he who turns our staffs into snakes and our inabilities into abilities. Instead we worry about how proficient or capable we appear. As Scottish theologian James Denny suggested, however: "No man can at the same time prove that he is clever and that Christ is mighty to save."[14]

Perhaps some of the most encouraging words about God's role in our competency comes from the story of Gideon, whom God called to save the Israelites from the Midianites. Gideon protested that not only was his clan the weakest, but that he was also the least in his family. Instead of letting Gideon wallow in his inadequacies, God told him to "go in the strength you have" (Judg. 6:14). Then we read that "the Spirit of the Lord came upon Gideon" (Judg. 6:34). The literal Hebrew meaning here is that the Spirit clothed himself with Gideon. Gideon simply became God's clothes. Talk about dressing for success! When we are willing to go in the strength we have, we too can become God's clothes.

What Are You Doing Here?
Our Need for Significance

Psychologists tell us that we are all in a neurotic pursuit of a sense of worth. Unfortunately, somewhere along the way someone decided that our significance should be based upon our achievements, that our value should come from what we do. Perhaps Elijah had fallen victim to this reasoning. We find him under a tree in 1 Kings 19:4 begging for the Lord to take his life because he had failed to restrain the wicked queen Jezebel and the poison she spewed against Israel.

Instead of reproaching Elijah for his failure, God asked him, "What are you doing here?" (1 Kings 19:9). God could have posed this question another way: "What is the meaning of life, Elijah? Is it based upon your victories or your failures? Is its essence found in how much you can accomplish? Do you think your worth is based upon what you do or don't do?"

Most of us have difficulty accepting that our significance is based upon who we are, not what we do. As image-bearers of God, we can know that we have infinite value and are worthy of respect and honor. We don't have to search for our significance: God has already given it to us. We just have to realize it.

Twelve Characteristics of Emotional Health

As we are able to know the identity, belonging, competence, and significance that is ours as Christians, we will see our lives marked by certain characteristics. Here is a discussion of one dozen of the qualities that flow from the life of someone who lives in the pink: self-awareness, flexibility, genuineness, generosity, intimacy, acceptance, humor, intrinsic orientation, commitment, purpose, responsibility, and expectancy.

Self-awareness. Of all God's creatures, only human beings are able to self-reflect, to think about who they are, how they feel, and why they feel that way. This self-awareness is the springboard to handling our emotions. Without it, we cannot experience spiritual growth because we have no concept of our spiritual condition. Self-awareness, then, is the foundation for change.

Self-awareness also involves an appreciation of how our attitudes and actions affect others. It is knowing the difference between how we see ourselves and how others see us. To do so requires that we be healthy enough to focus upon others instead of ourselves. If our relationships are based upon getting instead of giving, then we will be oblivious to the needs of others.

Most importantly, self-awareness allows us to see ourselves as God sees us. When we look into the mirror of God's eyes, we should see someone in need of grace, a sinner no better nor worse than anyone else. Self-awareness allows us to be convicted of our sin and to be humble about our salvation.

Flexibility. Babies, we are told, need routine and structure. They are happiest when they know what to expect and when to expect it, and they become upset when something upsets their way of life. Our daughter was in first grade before she stopped crying every time the furniture was rearranged. Our son used to insist that his toast be cut in quarters and that his pajamas have long sleeves. Unfortunately some of us never outgrow our intolerance for change.

"Many of us are crippled from birth," wrote Susan L. Lenzkes. "The backbone of our standard for living comes fused into unyielding rules and regulations. Then real life sneaks up and whacks us from behind, seeking to break our unbending back and our stiff neck, threatening to paralyze us."[15] Without flexibility we become rigid and stiff, incapable of growth. With it, we encourage growth not only in ourselves, but also in others as we free them to be themselves.

We become more flexible as we are able to lean back from situations and see them from a different perspective. As we realize that we are not the center of the universe, we become better equipped to understand that other people may not agree with our opinions and actions. Flexibility allows us not only to respect those who differ from us, but also to learn from them. It is the key to a generous and gracious life.

Genuineness. Writer Albert Camus suggested that man is the only creature who refuses to be what he is.[16] He wears a mask that smiles when he is actually frowning and that keeps a stiff upper lip when his is really pinched and puckered. One researcher, Richard Farson, estimated that millions of people in America have never had one minute in their lifetime where they could share their deepest feelings with another person.[17] We have become a nation of "I'm fine" fanatics who are not fine at all. Studies have shown that people who refuse to reveal themselves to others are the ones most at risk for emotional difficulties. Dr. Dean Ornish has suggested, "Anything that promotes a sense of isolation leads to chronic stress and, often, to illnesses."[18]

One reason we fail to be self-disclosing is that we fear rejection. To be genuine makes us vulnerable: the real me risks being rejected. Yet to love at all is to risk a part of ourselves. "Love anything, and your heart will certainly be wrung and possibly be broken. If you want to make sure of keeping it intact, you must give your heart to no one, not even an animal," wrote C. S. Lewis, who warned that "the only place outside heaven where you can be perfectly safe from all the dangers and perturbations of love is hell."[19]

Another reason for our lack of honesty in relationships is that we believe people will think the best of us if they see the best in us. However, people are actually put off and intimidated by those who mimic Barbie and Ken dolls. Because people are imperfect themselves, they are uncomfortable around someone who shows no imperfections. People identify not only with our strengths, but also with our weaknesses. Even Jesus, who was perfect, allowed his disciples to see him hurt. He shared his needs with them and wept openly.

At the opposite pole is Satan, who is perhaps the greatest pretender of all. The Bible tells us that despite his evil, he masquerades as an angel of light. "I am" is how God describes himself. Satan, however, would respond, "I am not."

Unless genuineness is part of our lives, we may as well be living someone else's life because we are not living our own.

Intimacy. From genuineness should flow another characteristic of health: intimacy. Alan Loy McGinnis suggested that the cardinal rule for developing intimacy is to dare to be needy.[20] People grow closest to us when we share our needs with them. If you want someone as a friend, ask her for a favor, advises an old adage. We all need to feel needed.

As we allow others into our lives, we will experience not just intimacy and meaningful relationships, but also emotional growth. When we keep others at surface level, we find that we know neither them nor ourselves. Sidney Jourard observed, "Every maladjusted person is a person who has not made himself known to another human being and in consequence does not know himself."[21]

Generosity. "It is one of the basic facts of human life that the ungiven self is the unfulfilled self," noted Harry and Bonaro Overstreet.[22] Those who live generous lives have learned the simple truth of Luke 6:38: when we give, it will be given to us. People who are generous with their encouragement, forgiveness, kindness, and patience realize rich and satisfying lives. Conversely, a selfish life is its own reward. "It is the individual who is not interested in his fellow man who has the greatest difficulties in life and provides the greatest injury to others. It is from among such individuals that all human failures spring," suggested well-known psychiatrist Alfred Adler.[23]

At times generosity may require us to place the needs of others above ourselves. It is in these moments that we discover how generous we truly are. Not only is self-sacrifice difficult, but it also is a virtue not highly regarded in a culture that exalts the self. Some psychologists contend that there is no such thing as self-sacrifice, and that any apparently self-sacrificial act has its own reward. This pessimistic stance ignores the deeper psychological and spiritual aspects of human beings. For the Christian, true self-sacrifice is not only possible, but it is also an expected manifestation of spiritual growth.

Generosity also implies that we are not just good givers, but also good receivers. We need to be able to graciously allow others to meet our needs. If you have an independent spirit that demands that you take nothing from anyone, you are keeping others from knowing the joy of giving. William James, considered to be the father of psychology, wrote, "The deepest principle in human nature is the craving to be appreciated."[24] By permitting others to give to us, we also give to them.

Humor. Many of us have trouble putting together humor and holiness. Somewhere we learned that to be reverent, we must be straight-faced and tight-lipped. We chastise our children when they giggle during prayers and scold them for silly behavior in church. Most of our paintings of Jesus show no hint of a smile. Yet humor is a sign of both spiritual wholeness and emotional health. Oswald Wynd has even suggested, "Laughter between two is sometimes a closer act of love than any other."[25]

The Bible says that God in his heaven laughs. Jesus often gave light-hearted and humorous replies. David danced gleefully before the Lord as an act of worship. Humor definitely will be part of heaven. We learn in the Beatitudes: "Blessed are you who weep now, for you will laugh" (Luke 6:21).

Humor is also important on earth. A keen sense of humor, wrote Billy Graham, "helps us to overlook the unbecoming, understand the unconventional, tolerate the unpleasant, overcome the unexpected, and outlast the unbearable."[26] Studies by Dr. Nick Stinnett and his associates reveal a close connection between humor and family strength. Funny remarks, family jokes, and playful attitudes are characteristic of stronger families. They are lacking in weaker families, Stinnett noted.[27]

Acceptance. There can be no friendship where there is no freedom, William Penn declared in 1693.[28] We might add that there can be no freedom where there is no acceptance. Unless we are willing to accept others as they are, we will not be able to give them the freedom to be themselves. We forever will try to mold them in our own image, to recreate them as we see fit.

The key to accepting others is found in the difference between two little words, *to* and *for*. We are responsible *to* others, but we are not responsible *for* others—not even for our spouse and children. While

God wants us to love, to build up, to honor, and to bear with others, he does not hold us responsible for how they respond to us. He does not command: "Thou shalt make thy mother happy. Thou shalt insure that thy child obeys. Thou shalt make thy spouse sober. Thou shalt dwell in my house forever if only thou keepest thy family safe and content." We are responsible for no one's actions and attitudes except our own because we cannot make anyone think, feel, or respond in a certain way.

Not only does our acceptance give others freedom, but it also brings freedom to us. When we quit trying to be personally responsible for someone else, we eliminate a great burden from our lives. Trying to control other people is a lot of work.

Acceptance means realizing that other people will fail us. It means realizing that because other people are no more perfect than we are, we should not take to heart their every comment or action against us. It means allowing some things to bounce off our backs: thoughtless remarks, unfounded criticisms, unrealistic expectations. When we accept others, we accept their weaknesses as well as their strengths. Acceptance allows us to be strong enough to withstand the actions of imperfect people without being overcome. It allows us to forgive them for not being perfect.

Perhaps the imperfect person we have the most difficulty accepting is ourselves. "We have to make peace with our limitations," warned Harold Lindsell.[29] When we don't, we spend our lives kicking ourselves for our shortcomings and worrying about our next blunder. One of the greatest gifts we can give ourselves is forgiveness for not being perfect.

Accepting ourselves means acknowledging that we

are saved by God's grace, that we cannot earn his approval. Accepting others requires us to remember that everyone swims in the same pool of grace. As a result, we are free to forgive both ourselves and other individuals who fall beneath our expectations.

Intrinsic orientation. This area concerns our motivations in life. Those who are intrinsically oriented live from the inside out. Their motivation comes from a heart-felt desire to please God, not to gain the appreciation of others. They are able to follow Christ's command to do good works in secrecy because their desire is to give, not to get.

Extrinsically motivated people, by contrast, give out of a need for profit. Their love for God is like their love for a cow, explained Meister Eckhart in the thirteenth century. "You love it for the sake of its milk and cheese."[30] Those who have extrinsic motivations are more concerned with pleasing or impressing others than with pleasing God. Jesus used the Pharisees as an example: they appeared generous but did everything from selfish motives. "You are like whitewashed tombs, which look beautiful on the outside but on the inside are full of dead men's bones and everything unclean," he warned them in Matthew 23:27.

When our work stems from intrinsic motivation, it takes on an element of spirituality not present when our motivation is external. When we serve wholeheartedly, as if we are serving the Lord and not men (Eph. 6:7), whatever we do becomes meaningful. "Religion consists, not so much in doing spiritual or sacred acts, as in doing secular acts from a sacred or religious motive," said Scottish pastor John Caird in 1855.[31] Whether we care for an aged parent or mop the floor, we can glorify God through the intrinsic motivation behind our action.

Commitment. "To dare to make and care to keep commitments—this is to live," wrote Lewis Smedes in *Caring & Commitment*.[32] While commitments may not always be pleasant or convenient to maintain, they reflect our willingness to put others first in our life, to give even when we are not getting. In a society that cries, "Me first!" commitment has been one of the first casualties. We live in a world that makes it easy for us to give up on other people and ourselves.

As we keep our commitments, however, we reflect on earth a bit of God's faithfulness. We help others to know their importance. Whether our commitment is to take a daughter to lunch or to return a neighbor's book, we do well when we follow through on our promises.

Purpose. Dennis and Barbara Rainey wrote that Helen Keller was once asked, "Is there anything worse than being blind?" "Yes," she replied, "The most pathetic person in the whole world is someone who has sight but has no vision."[33]

Some of us are so busy living that we have no sense of life. The good news is that we are making great time; the bad news is that we don't know where we are going. The Christian with such narrow vision leads a cautious, protective, self-centered existence that lacks meaning and mission.

Without purpose, we risk not only an unfulfilled life, but also illness. "The diseases peculiar to man . . . have something to do with a malaise that is specific to man: the feeling that his life is not attaining its fullness.

For to man alone is life given as a task to be fulfilled. If a man does not fulfill his task, then death supervenes," wrote Paul Tournier.[34] Life must be about more than living; we each must find and fulfill our God-given role in creation.

Responsibility. Taking responsibility for our actions, feelings, and choices takes courage and maturity. How much easier it is to lay the blame for them at the feet of another. We can always find an excuse, whether we fault our upbringing, our society, our dysfunctional environment, another's provocation, or our state of mind. Like David, we need to confess, "I know my transgressions. . . . Create in me a pure heart" (Ps. 51:3, 10). When we take responsibility for our failings, we free ourselves to be justified by faith, not by excuses. When we admit no fault, however, we can accept no pardon.

Expectancy. A. Antonovsky has suggested that people stay healthy because they have developed a "sense of coherence" or confidence about how things will turn out in the world. Healthy people, he wrote, believe that things will probably work out as well as can be expected.[35]

Christians, then, should be the most expectant people of all: we have already read the end of the book, and we know how things work out. We know not only that we are headed for a world where we will fully realize God's love, but also that, despite whatever sorrows today brings, God, in all his glory, is present. We must therefore embrace today expectantly, actively looking for the wonders of God wherever circumstances find us. Because we are alive in Christ, we must awaken our souls to the joy inherent in each day. God is with us.

Notes

Introduction
Color Me Fascinated

[1]Carole Jackson, *Color Me Beautiful* (Washington, D.C.: Acropolis, 1980).

Chapter 1
Understanding Our Colorful Emotions

[1]While psychologists have been debating the nature of emotion for years, the debate is far from resolved. Our position is "primacy of cognition," which states that human emotion is primarily the product of thinking, perception, belief, and appraisal.

[2]While we believe Jesus felt every basic emotion, certain feelings (such as rage, envy, and bitterness) go beyond basic reactions and are classified as nurtured and sinful emotions. Clearly Jesus experienced no sinful emotions.

[3]Rochelle S. Albin, *Emotions* (Philadelphia: Westminster, 1983).

Chapter 2
Discovering Our Emotional Colors

[1]The "Emotional Color Analysis" is not a formal psychological test. Its items are drawn from the content of chapters four through eleven, but they have not been subjected to reliability or validity studies.

Chapter 3
Changing Our Colors

[1]Flanders Dunbar, *Emotions and Bodily Changes* (New York: Columbia Univ. Press, 1954). Although almost thirty years old, this book continues to be cited by recent researchers in the *Science Citation Index*.

[2]Virginia O'Leary, "Women, Men, and Emotion" (Presented at the 1988 annual convention of the American Psychological Association, Atlanta).

[3]Richard J. Foster, *Celebration of Discipline: The Path to Spiritual Growth*, rev. ed. (San Francisco: Harper & Row, 1988).

Chapter 4
Seeing Red for Right and Wrong Reasons—Anger

[1]Quoted by Franklin M. Segler, *Your Emotions and Your Faith* (Nashville: Broadman, 1970), 67.

[2]Quoted by James W. Angell, *Learning to Manage Our Fears* (Nashville: Abingdon, 1981), 57.

[3]Quoted by Segler, *Your Emotions and Your Faith*, 72.

[4]Richard S. Lazarus, *Emotion and Adaptation* (New York: Oxford Univ. Press, 1991).

[5]Louisa M. Alcott, *Little Women* (Cleveland: World Publishing, 1946), 100.

[6]Mary Ellen Ashcroft, *Temptations Women Face* (Downers Grove, Ill.: InterVarsity Press, 1991), 104.

[7]N. K. Hayles, "Anger in Different Voices: Carol Gilligan and the 'Mill on the Floss,'" *Signs* 12 (1986): 39.

[8]Teresa Bernardez-Bonesatti is quoted by Harriet Lerner in "The Taboos Against Female Anger," a paper distributed at a 1988 workshop, "Dealing with Feelings," at Pine Rest Christian Hospital, Grand Rapids, Mich., by Jorie Fikkert-Mitchell.

[9]Redford Williams, "Curing Type A, The Trusting Heart," *Psychology Today* (January/February 1989).

Notes

[10]Virginia O'Leary, "Women, Men, and Emotion," (Presented at the 1988 annual convention of the American Psychological Association, Atlanta).

[11]Lerner, "The Taboos Against Female Anger."

[12]Quoted in "How Anger Leads to Illness," *McLennan County Mental Health Association Newsletter* 4, no. 3 (1990): 4.

[13]Lloyd J. Ogilvie, *Making Stress Work for You: Ten Proven Principles* (Waco, Tex.: Word, 1984), 43.

[14]Quoted by Lewis Smedes, *Forgive & Forget: Healing the Hurts We Don't Deserve* (New York: Pocket Books, 1984), 12.

[15]Sidney M. Jourard, *The Transparent Self,* rev. ed. (New York: Van Nostrand Reinhold, 1971).

[16]Les Carter, *Good 'n' Angry: How to Handle Your Anger Positively* (Grand Rapids: Baker, 1983), 35.

[17]William Penn, *Some Fruits of Solitude,* 1693.

Chapter 5
Feeling Blue When We Experience Loss—Sadness

[1]The relationship between stress and loss is documented in *The Social Readjustment Rating Scale (SRRS),* Holmes & Rahe, 1967.

[2]Richard S. Lazarus, *Emotion and Adaptation* (New York: Oxford Univ. Press, 1991).

[3]Max Gates, "Researchers zero in on causes of depression in baby boomers," *The Grand Rapids Press* (June 4, 1989): B5.

[4]William Walter Warmath, *Our God Is Able* (Nashville: Broadman, 1967), 101.

[5]Mary Jane Worden, *NIV Women's Devotional Bible* (Grand Rapids: Zondervan, 1990), 794.

[6]Charles H. Spurgeon, *The Treasury of Spurgeon* (Grand Rapids: Baker, 1967), 45.

[7]Dorothy Sayers, *Creed or Chaos?* (New York: Harcourt, Brace, and Co., 1949), 4.

[8]Arthur T. Pierson quoted by Mrs. Charles E. Cowman, *Streams in the Desert* (Los Angeles: The Oriental Missionary Society, 1925), 313.

[9]Harvey Kiekover, "From 'Whys' to Works," *The Banner* (February 13, 1989): 5.

Chapter 6
A Purple Rage—Bitterness and Depression

[1]S. I. McMillen, *None of These Diseases* (Charlotte: Commission, 1979, reprinted with permission from Fleming H. Revell), 72.

[2]Benjamin J. Stein, "How to Live Another Year," *Reader's Digest* (November 1991): 152.

[3]Smedes, *Forgive & Forget*, 12.

[4]David W. Augsburger, *Seventy Times Seven: The Freedom of Forgiveness* (Chicago: Moody Press, 1970), 20.

[5]Quoted by Bergan Evans, *Dictionary of Quotations* (New York: Delacorte, 1968), 248.

[6]Paul Meier, in the forward of *Good 'n' Angry: How to Handle Your Anger Positively* by Les Carter (Grand Rapids: Baker, 1983), 5.

[7]Max Gates, "Researchers zero in on causes of depression in baby boomers," *The Grand Rapids Press* (June 4, 1989): B5.

[8]Adrian P. Rogers, *Mastering Your Emotions* (Nashville: Broadman, 1988), 27.

[9]Daniel Goleman, "Depressed people lack 'thought-cleansing' ability, study finds," *The Grand Rapids Press* (December 1, 1988): D13.

Chapter 7
A Streak of Yellow—Fear

[1]David Wallechinsky, Irving Wallace, and Amy Wallace, *People's Almanac Presents the Book of Lists* (New York: William Morrow, 1977), 469.

Notes

[2]Quoted by James W. Angell, *Learning to Manage Our Fears* (Nashville: Abingdon, 1981), 57.

[3]"I Was Raped . . . ," *Woman's Day* (February 14, 1989): 154.

[4]Quoted by William S. Walsh, *International Encyclopedia of Prose and Poetical Quotations* (New York: Greenwood, 1968), 1045.

[5]David Burns, *Feeling Good: The New Mood Therapy* (New York: Morrow, 1980).

[6]Quoted by Angell, *Learning to Manage Our Fears*, 11.

[7]Ira Dreyfuss, "A vigorous workout is a distraction for worries," *The Waco Tribune-Herald* (April 4, 1992), 1B.

[8]*Woman's Day* (June 2, 1992), 28.

[9]Quoted in Sharlene King, "How to feel better about the future," *Ladies' Home Journal* (May 1992): 94.

[10]Quoted by Angell, *Learning to Manage Our Fears*, 77.

[11]Quoted by Tony Castle, *The New Book of Christian Quotations* (New York: Crossroad, 1982), F210.

[12]"The Secret Life of Howard Hughes," *Time Magazine* (December 13, 1976), 22–41.

[13]John Tallach, *God Made Them Great* (Carlisle, Pa.: The Banner of Truth Trust, 1974), 27.

[14]Haldor Lillenas, *Modern Gospel Song Stories* (Kansas City: Lillenas Publishing, 1952), 84–85.

[15]William Sadler, *Practice of Psychiatry* (St. Louis: C. V. Mosby, 1953), 1012–13.

[16]Both descriptions of worry are quoted by William Walter Warmath, *Our God Is Able* (Nashville: Broadman, 1967), 111–12.

[17]Ralph Waldo Emerson, *Society and Solitude, Twelve Chapters* (Boston: Houghton, Mifflin & Co., 1870), 161–68.

Chapter 8
How Turning Green Brings Double Trouble—Envy

[1]Billy Graham, *Seven Deadly Sins* (Grand Rapids: Zondervan, 1955), 41–42.

[2]The story by Count Lev Nikolayevich Tolstoy is given by

Charles L. Allen, *God's Psychiatry* (Old Tappan, N.J.: Fleming H. Revell, 1953), 80.

[3]Quoted by Lloyd J. Ogilvie, *Making Stress Work for You* (Waco, Tex.: Word, 1984), 104.

[4]C. S. Lewis, *Mere Christianity* (New York: MacMillan, 1943), 109.

[5]Maggie Kane, "I felt like I had lost my life," *Parade* (April 7, 1991): 25.

[6]S. I. McMillen, *None of These Diseases*, 128.

[7]Paul B. Maves, ed., *The Church and Mental Health* (New York: Charles Scribner's Sons, 1953), 17.

[8]This story was shared with us by Steve and Dee Larkin, who are unfamiliar with its author.

[9]Tony Campolo, *Seven Deadly Sins* (Wheaton, Ill.: Victor, 1987), 101.

[10]Monica Furlong, *Christian Uncertainties* (Cambridge: Cowley, 1975), 35.

Chapter 9
When We Are Driven by the Orange Flames—Urgency

[1]Quoted by Eleanor Doan, *Speakers Sourcebook* (Grand Rapids: Zondervan, 1960), 44.

[2]Karen S. Peterson, "There's no way to beat the clock," *USA Today* (April 13, 1989): 1D.

[3]Randy Kraft, "Weekend leisure time in danger: hotel survey," *The Grand Rapids Press* (March 12, 1989): G1.

[4]"Problems of 'pace addiction' analyzed," *The Waco Tribune-Herald* (December 26, 1991): 7C.

[5]Nina Tassi, "Stop Racing the Clock!" *Working Mother* (April 1992): 68.

[6]Jean Fleming, *Between Walden and the Whirlwind* (Colorado Springs: NavPress, 1984), 13–14.

[7]Mark R. Littleton, "Time Out!" *Moody Monthly* (May 1989): 19.

[8]Power Publications, Box 9009, Tyler TX 75711-9009.

[9]Jean Fleming, "How Busy Is Too Busy?" *Decision* (March 1988): 17.

[10]Quoted by Foster, *Celebration of Discipline*, 15.

[11]Billy Graham, *Hope for the Troubled Heart* (Dallas: Word, 1991), 187.

[12]A. M. Pines, E. Aronson, and D. Kafry, *Burnout: From Tedium to Personal Growth* (New York: Free Press, 1981), 3.

[13]Jay Conrad Levinson, quoted by Stephanie Culp, *Streamlining Your Life* (Cincinnati: Writer's Digest Books, 1991), 98.

[14]"Sniffles and Stress," *Working Mother* (February 1992): 28.

[15]Quoted by Doan, *Speakers Sourcebook*, 280.

[16]Mark Porter, *The Time of Your Life* (Wheaton, Ill.: Victor, 1983), 36.

[17]Henry David Thoreau, *Walden and Other Writings* (New York: Bantam, 1962), 132–33.

[18]Imelda Marcos, quoted by Stephanie Culp, *Streamlining Your Life*, 92.

[19]Ivern Ball, quoted by Stephanie Culp, *Streamlining Your Life*, 75.

[20]John Milton, "On his Blindness."

[21]Henry Kissinger, quoted by Stephanie Culp, *Streamlining Your Life*, 58.

[22]William Walter Warmath, *Our God Is Able* (Nashville: Broadman, 1967), 44.

[23]Marlene LeFever, "Confessions of a Compulsive Time Manager," *Today's Christian Woman* (September/October 1989): 46.

[24]Elizabeth Barrett Browning, "Aurora Leigh."

[25]Henri J. M. Nouwen, *The Way of the Heart* (New York: Ballantine, 1981), 17.

[26]Thomas S. Kepler, ed., *Selections from the Writings of François Fenelon* (Nashville, Tenn.: The Upper Room, 1962), 9.

[27]Mark Twain, quoted by Stephanie Culp, *Streamlining Your Life*, 42.

[28]Judy Seabaugh, "Is My Heart in Stable Condition?" *Decision* (December 1988): 39.

29Mark Porter, *The Time of Your Life*, 9.
30Quoted by Graham, *Hope for the Troubled Heart*, 163.

Chapter 10
When Black Darkens Our World—Guilt

1"Judgment Call," reprinted in *Reader's Digest* (May 1992): 71.
2Quoted in the *Waco Tribune Herald* (June 29, 1992): 2A.
3C. S. Lewis, *Mere Christianity* (New York: MacMillan, 1943), 38–39.
4Quoted in David Seamands, *Healing for Damaged Emotions* (Wheaton, Ill.: Victor, 1988), 29.
5Les Carter, *Mind Over Emotions* (Grand Rapids: Baker, 1985), 75.
6John T. McNeill, ed., *Calvin: Institutes of the Christian Religion*, book 3, chapter 3, section 2 (Philadelphia: Westminster, 1960), 594.
7David Heller, *The Children's God* (Chicago: The Univ. of Chicago Press, 1986).

Chapter 11
Living in the Pink

1Richard S. Lazarus, *Emotion and Adaptation* (New York: Oxford Univ. Press, 1991).
2R. Veenhoven, *How Harmful Is Happiness?* (Rotterdam: Universitaire Pers Rotterdam, 1990).
3Vernon C. Grounds, "The Importance of Glorifying God: Eight Thoughts on Mental Health," *Christianity Today* (January 17, 1986): 28.
4David G. Brenner, "Toward a Psychology of Spirituality: Implications for Personality and Psychotherapy," *Journal of Psychology and Christianity* 8, no. 1 (1989): 25.
5Kenneth L. Woodward, "Why America Prays," *Reader's Digest* (April 1992): 198.

Notes

[6]Carl Jung, *Modern Man in Search of a Soul* (New York: Harcourt, Brace, & Co., 1933), 178.

[7]Brenner, "Toward a Psychology of Spirituality," 25.

[8]C. Stephen Evans, "The Blessings of Mental Anguish," *Christianity Today* (January 17, 1986): 27.

[9]A. van Kamm, *On Being Yourself* (Denvill, N.J.: Dimension Books, 1972).

[10]Ruth Bell Graham, "His Brother's Brother," *NIV Women's Devotional Bible* (Grand Rapids: Zondervan, 1990), 7.

[11]Eric L. Johnson, "Self-Esteem in the Presence of God," *Journal of Psychology and Theology* 17, no. 3 (1989): 228.

[12]John H. Westerhoff, *Will Our Children Have Faith?* (New York: Seabury, 1976), 36.

[13]John Bowlby, *Attachment and Loss,* vol. 3 of *Sadness and Depression* (New York: Basic, 1980).

[14]Quoted by Lloyd J. Ogilvie, *If God Cares, Why Do I Still Have Problems?* (Waco, Tex.: Word, 1985), 208.

[15]Susan L. Lenzkes, "Flexible Living," *NIV Women's Devotional Bible* (Grand Rapids: Zondervan, 1990), 192.

[16]Quoted by Bruce Larson, *Believe and Belong* (Old Tappan, N.J.: Fleming H. Revell, 1982), 45.

[17]Alan Loy McGinnis, *The Friendship Factor: How to Get Closer to the People You Care for* (Minneapolis: Augsburg, 1979), 11.

[18]Dean Ornish, "The Healing Power of Love," *Prevention* (February 1991): 62.

[19]C. S. Lewis, *The Four Loves* (San Diego: Harcourt Brace Jovanovich, 1969), 169.

[20]McGinnis, *The Friendship Factor,* 123.

[21]Jourard, *The Transparent Self,* 32.

[22]Quoted in Harry J. Johnson, *Blue Print for Health* (Chicago: Blue Cross Assoc., 1962), 19.

[23]Quoted in McMillen, *None of These Diseases,* 77.

[24]Quoted in Dennis and Barbara Rainey, *Building Your Mate's Self-Esteem* (San Bernardino: Here's Life, 1986), 107.

[25]Oswald Wynd, quoted in *Reader's Digest* (July 1992): 118.

[26]Graham, *Hope for the Troubled Heart*, 188.

[27]*Woman's Day* (June 2, 1992): 28.

[28]William Penn, *Some Fruits of Solitude*, 1693.

[29]Quoted by Doan, *Speakers Sourcebook*, 220.

[30]Quoted by Anne Ortlund, *Disciplines of the Heart: Tuning Your Inner Life to God* (Waco, Tex.: Word, 1987), 70.

[31]Grenville Kleiser, comp., *The World's Great Sermons*, vol. 6 (London: Funk and Wagnalls, 1908), 171–72.

[32]Lewis Smedes, *Caring & Commitment: Learning to Live the Love We Promise* (San Francisco: Harper & Row, 1988), 153.

[33]Rainey, *Building Your Mate's Self-Esteem*, 189.

[34]Paul Tournier, expressing the views of Professor Arthur Jores in *Learn to Grow Old* (New York: Harper & Row, 1971), 163.

[35]A. Antonovsky, *Unraveling the Mystery of Health: How People Manage Stress and Stay Well* (San Francisco: Jossey-Bass, 1987).

About the Authors

Why do God's children experience so many negative feelings? This question was the motivation for writing *Seeing Red, Feeling Blue, or in the Pink*. Tonya Pantle began studying and researching emotions six years ago, presenting much of the material in this book to her church, Hillside Community, in Grand Rapids, Michigan. With the help of her husband, a clinical psychologist, she brought these ideas to print.

With a master's degree in journalism, Tonya currently is a doctoral student and research assistant in education at Baylor University. A working journalist since the age of sixteen, she has published articles and photographs in a variety of newspapers and magazines. In addition to her lectures on emotions, she also has presented seminars and workshops on relationships, decision-making, and self-esteem.

Mark Pantle, Ph.D., is a licensed clinical psychologist, an assistant professor of psychology at Baylor University, and a member of the academic medical staff of Pine Rest Christian Hospital in Grand Rapids, Michigan. He has written for psychology and psychiatry journals and has presented papers and workshops at national conferences.

Tonya and Mark reside in a four-generation home in Waco, Texas, with their two children, Joelle and Matthew, and Tonya's parents and grandmother.